DEPROGRAMMING VICTIMS OF BRAINWASHING AND CULT-LIKE MIND CONTROL

METHODS YOU CAN APPLY

Deprogramming Victims of Brainwashing and Cult-Like Mind Control

COPYRIGHT © 2020 Prism S. Thomas

All rights reserved

G STEMPIEN PUBLISHING COMPANY

ISBN 978-0-930472-47-4

Editorial offices in New Quay, Wales, UK

The activities taken in this book were successful for the author. The outcome cannot be guaranteed when used in any other situation. Medical advice of any type is not implied.

PB

CONTENTS

FOREWORD

PART 1
HOW CONTROL IS TAKEN

1. Introduction
2. Stages of Control
3. The Enemy
4. The First Warning Signs
5. Triggers of Control
6. Hypnosis vs. Brainwashing
7. The Assault on the Support Group
8. Weapon of Silence
9. Hacking a Relationship
10. Other Causes of Departure
11. Gone
12. Forcing a Response
13. In Person Assault
14. The Brainwashing Suite
15. Pledge of Guilt

16. Sex is Control

17. A Sound Torture

18. False Victories/Escapes

19. I Become You

20. Fake "Gurus" & "Spiritual Leaders"

PART 2
REVERSAL/RECOVERY

1. Introduction
2. Reclaiming A Relationship
3. Revealing Hypnotic Control
4. Changing the Tune
5. Exposing An Enemy
6. Breaking the Grip of Sex
7. You Become I Again
8. Stalemate
9. Confound the Enemy
10. The Final Stage

APPENDIX 1

CRISIS POINTS DURING THE EARLY STAGES OF MIND CONTROL AND WHAT YOU CAN DO

APPENDIX 2

GUIDE TO RECOVERY AND REVERSAL METHODS FOR IMMEDIATE USE

FOREWORD

A loved one, friend or associate of yours has become ensnared in a cult, secret society, organized hate group or other powerful association and you don't understand how it happened. Your friend or loved one is using terms you've never heard before, acting strangely and has become like another person. You suspect that he or she has been brainwashed and you are confused and mystified and have no idea what to do. You are left in total confusion and feel helpless and alone.

This book will explain what has happened and it will describe the process of brainwashing. It will also instruct you how to reverse the effects of brainwashing. This will be done in plain, everyday language and will not be couched in confusing scientific terms.

This is not about theory or speculation. It is about practical methods of deprogramming victims of brainwashing that work and can be applied by any average adult.

PART 1

HOW CONTROL IS TAKEN

INTRODUCTION

Mind control and brainwashing are procedures that can be performed by anyone who has the proper information. They are not magic or beyond common understanding As such, the effects of mind control and brainwashing can be undone by anyone who has the knowledge of how to do so. Supplying this knowledge is what this book is about.

This is a detailed instruction book to be used like a manual to counter the effects of mind control methods such as hypnosis and brainwashing. You will be able to free the mind of a person or persons who have come under the subversive control of another, be this assailant the head of a "spiritual cult," the leader of a hate group or even the single abuser who uses his will to dominate a single targeted individual. The methods of control by these exploiters are basically the same and these methods can be overcome in basically the same way.

You have probably already sought help elsewhere. And you have probably already found that there is little to none available on this topic. Experts who can deprogram victims of mind control are difficult if not impossible to locate. You may even have lost hope, but hope does exist.

In order to receive the most reliable information about deprogramming victims of mind control it is important for the person supplying this information to have experience in brainwashing. Not simple behavior modification, but actual brainwashing. I have that experience, gained through NSA activity. My credentials in this subject area are by direct experience.

While none of the information that follows is classified, it is seldom encountered in ordinary daily life and, in that, it is specialized knowledge, although it can be freely disseminated. All of the procedures that will be revealed can be put into practice by the average citizen with proper instruction.

This author has direct experience battling and overcoming the type of egomaniac who uses mind control to dominate – subjugate – others to his will. What you are about to be shown is not theory or experiment, it is a tested process. In order to deprogram someone it is important to know how they were programmed or brainwashed.

Deprogramming does not mean overlaying your own fashion of brainwashing over that which was imposed by another source. Deprogramming unwinds the bindings of control that have been wound around the victim's thoughts and is a methodical way of removing this previous negative binding influence. Again – deprogramming is not installing one form of brainwashing for another form of brainwashing. Brainwashing in ANY form is unethical.

This book will demonstrate how to deprogram a victim of mind control. There is hope, although, you should expect a battle – often a long battle – but one which should have a positive outcome. How long will this battle take? It is impossible to give a specific time frame. Partly it depends on how deeply the victim who you are trying to free is submerged in the powers of the subjugator.

But from my experience and other peoples' experiences, it often requires about 15 months in general to clear a person of mind control to the point where they can function freely.

This may sound like a long time – but people who are left under control of the subjugator often never escape him.

The type of hypnosis and brainwashing that is considered in these pages is not of the highly technical variety that governmental intelligence agencies apply or the type usually shown on television or at the movies where powerful drugs are often administered to the victim along with other physical measures of manipulation. That is beyond the scope of this book, and probably any book. The common cult or secret organization undertakes mind control of a cruder nature but which is nevertheless ruthless and highly effective, sometimes relying on the use of more common drugs like LSD and ketamine. This is what will be dealt with in this book.

Consider what our intelligence agencies do when one of our operatives is returned after having been brainwashed by the other side. He is deprogrammed. But how? What happens is that the methods that were used to brainwash the individual are identified and these procedures are broken down and removed in a systematic technique. That is what will be done in this book on a less sophisticated level. In order to remove these binding controls it must be understood what they are and how they were imposed. That is why so much time will be spent on describing the specific techniques used in performing brainwashing. Then they can be removed.

In the first part of the book specific instances of mind control with which this author has personally dealt will be related. The recounting of the affair extends from the beginning stages, through the depths of subjugation, to the conclusion and afterwards (however, this is not a life story). A prime purpose in revealing the entire length of the brainwashing event that is the example used here is to allow you to gauge by comparison how deeply the victim in your situation is under the control of the manipulator.

Not all episodes of mind control need run their full course and they can be derailed in mid progress. Some may even be halted before becoming critical of nature. It is important to understand the entire process of this deep form of behavior control.

Throughout this book, special **CRISIS POINTS**, will be highlighted at the moment of occurrence and will be noted in the first appendix. This is to alert you to highly dangerous strategic moments during the mind control process which are of critical importance, where action on your part to counter it is vital and could be definitive. If you notice that what is happening between you and a victim you are attempting to defend is the same activity that is occurring at one of these crisis points be aware and take action. Strategies for neutralizing the techniques used in mind control will be shown in part 2 of this book and can be applied by most people.

A few terms are helpful to know at the start. Brainwashing is when a victim's subconscious is taken control of by an outside party and ruthlessly subverted in such a way as to entirely destroy his will and subjugate it to the attacker. Throughout this book the descriptions – victim and subjugator – will be used often. As related to you, the victim can be either a close friend, loved one, spouse or significant other. The subjugator is the person who seeks to control the victim. The person who will deprogram the victim – probably you – is referred to as the defender.

There is a definite pattern of how a person is placed under control and describing it is where we will start. But remember in all of this, the final outcome of deprogramming must be directed toward what is in the VICTIM'S own best interest which may not be the same conclusion which you would prefer to see.

Stages of Control

As already noted, the basic format in enforcing mind control is essentially the same in all cases. This follows specific stages of manipulation that are generally copied in all instances. Knowing these stages and using them as guidelines in **deconstructing** the subjugator's application of mind control will be the primary weapon in freeing the mind of the victim.

The basic stages in gaining control of a mind are the following: 1). Removing the victim from his or her support group. At first psychologically then physically. The support group includes friends, family or **ANYONE** who the victim can be influenced by. 2). Attack of the victim's self esteem and convincing him or her that he or she has a mental or spiritual problem which only the subjugator can cure with his special abilities. 3). Forcing the victim to perform menial tasks of a humiliating and degrading nature, potentially including the performance of sexual activity with the subjugator who has convinced his captive that he alone can ever fulfill her or his erotic needs and that celibacy is required with everyone but him. 4). Blatantly sadistic abuse both physically and psychologically. 5). The transfer of most or all of the victim's finances to the control of the subjugator which gives him absolute control of the victim from which the captive cannot escape because his or her funds now belong to the subjugator.

With each stage, the victim's power to resist becomes weaker and weaker and the control wielded by the subjugator becomes stronger. This, however, can be interrupted at any point.

If you are trying at this moment to free a person from another's control consider the 5 steps just outlined and determine where along that scale of domination the victim should be placed. This will let you know how deeply he or she is under the subjugator's control. While the 5 stages can vary slightly, the final result will be the same if left unchecked.

In part 2 of this book you will be instructed on how to intervene at each stage. In order to be effective, you must first know how these stages of control were forced upon the victim, and that is what follows. First, you must determine who the true enemy is because there is only **ONE** source of the brainwashing.

The Enemy

Why an enemy? Must there be AN enemy? In this case, yes, there must. In general, I do not like the term "enemy" but in matters of mind manipulation it must be recognized that there is one person in control of this process because he or she alone **MUST** be deprived of all such power in order to free the victim. Neither the subjugator's associates nor his enablers, nor anyone else following his orders can take his place; and depriving them of their power will not have any effect on the leader.

The leader alone must be stopped and denied the ability to impose more acts of mental and even spiritual cruelty. Remember, the control he is wielding upon the person you are attempting to free has already been imposed upon his followers and enablers. None of them can be trusted to help you or the victim! They are pledged to serve the master.

The subjugator – no matter his title – is your target and the **ONLY** target in regards to ending the the source of mind control! Focusing on his supporters would only be a distraction which will not diminish his strength or help the victim who is struggling under his control like an innocent in a spider's web.

Who is this enemy on a personal level? He is an egomaniacal, psychopathic narcissist. He is a person who is devoid of a conscience, has no concern or feeling for anyone else except himself and believes that he has unlimited powers and abilities. In most cases he truly has far above average intelligence but uses this intellect for deceitful and destructive purposes.

Basically, he is a master **CON MAN**. He is usually a person of great charm and charisma – not necessarily handsome or cultured – who can beguile his victims into believing he is a warm, caring and honest individual even though he is in reality hateful and ruthless. The subjugator is usually described as a wonderful, loving, highly attractive person by his victims in almost all cases where mind control is concerned. That is the **DELUSION** he has implanted into their psyches.

As noted, the leader of a cult, secret organization or other type of control group often has a genius level intellect.

This should not daunt anyone because despite his IQ, he is potentially insane and can be victimized by his own ego. And, keep in mind, one of the best weapons against him will be confusion, not just any type of confusion but a special type. A confusion based on conflicting cues that the defender – you, the person trying to save the victim – will present to the subjugator at the proper time, keeping him bewildered as to your true relationship to the situation as a whole. In other words make the subjugator uncertain whether or not you, the defender, supports him and his ideology. This is the type of conundrum that will keep his thought pattern in knots.

This person – the subjugator – will remain the enemy throughout the deprogramming process and beyond. He will never admit defeat. He will always be lurking, ready to regain control and there is always the possibility that some of his brainwashing triggers will be activated even after the victim escapes. However, in reality after the victim's flight it may be nearly impossible for the subjugator to have any additional effect on him.

But beware, the subjugator has terrified the victim into believing he can wage his assaults whenever he chooses. This is a delusion that is very difficult to extinguish and is a common practice used by pimps to keep their girls under control. In fact, pimps are among the subjugators who are targeted in this book.

Remember, the major tool of the subjugator is brainwashing. This is in conjunction with hypnosis. The difference between the two will be studied in detail shortly and it is critical to understand.

Brainwashing can produce severe and bizarre effects. One effect is to cause the victim to physically view the subjugator according to his own description of himself. Handsome, strong, virile, potent, godly – even though he is usually the exact opposite. Note the physical appearances of these cult leaders: David Koresh (Branch Davidian), James Jones (People's Temple) and Marshall Applewhite Jr. (Heaven's Gate). None of these 3 were particularly attractive. But they convinced there female victims that they were. And the males in the group saw them as godly and powerful. Of course, the 3 cult leaders mentioned did possess that special trait common to charismatic personalities.

So, if the subjugator with whom you are struggling may not appear to be as handsome or as powerful as the victim claims, keep in mind that she sees him through **HIS** eyes as he wants to be seen. The author has experienced the erroneous result of this delusion often. In one case, during a preliminary meeting, a photograph was shown to me of the subjugator to whom the victim was hopelessly attracted. It revealed such a weak and mousy figure that it was difficult to keep from laughing. One matter prevented any laughter – he also was clearly insane. His madness was very obviously portrayed in the depths behind his eyes. Body and facial language are other areas of my research. ("Analyze Anyone on Sight – for the 21st Century" and "Micro-expressions: Reading Anyone's Hidden Thoughts").

Following up on the above observation, the subjugator will use his mind control techniques to make you look as unattractive as possible to the victim – both physically and personally. That is a critical part of his procedure in convincing the victim to sever ties with you, whatever these ties may be, including marriage. He must make you appear as a despicable, loathsome and untrustworthy person to the victim and he has the ability to accomplish this. He will also induce paranoia, causing the victim to believe that you and others in her support group are conspiring against her.

The subjugator's appeal is not generally to the slow-witted or uneducated individual. Many intelligent and highly successful people are fooled into accepting the dominion of this type of con man. For example, from as far back as the 1830's a fake preacher calling himself Matthias the Prophet swindled many thousands of dollars from several prominent New York businessmen by convincing them that he was the incarnation of God on earth. Not only did they give him a large part of their fortunes but their wives as well.

What could possibly convince intelligent people to act so recklessly? One answer is that these people – even though successful in life – suffered from having highly addictive personalities. Those who accept the preaching of a person who claims to have special, super powers are inclined to be the types who – once in the trap – become addicted to the person who set the trap and are willing to accept any dogma and any delusion he provides. Addiction to another human being is a very real psychological condition and is the basis for many people's mindless attraction and subservience to a subjugator.

And that is one of the most important reasons why the subjugator must be focused upon as the only enemy – and perhaps the most important reason – because he will be the figure with whom the victim will become addicted. It is partially this addiction which will keep the victim bound by mental imprisonment.

THE FIRST WARNING SIGNS
Obsessive fixation on a specific topic
A CHANCE TO INTERVENE

The potential victim is obsessed with an idea, person, or both, to the exclusion of ALL ELSE.

This is monomania. Monomaniacal behavior will usually be the first thing you will notice which reveals that a critical problem exists. Monomania is an old-fashioned term but I prefer it because it is to the point and is very descriptive. Monomania is when a person is obsessed with an idea or a person, or both, to the exclusion of everything else. Sometimes a victim may incessantly repeat an activity over and over again to the point of absurdity but this isn't common in the situation that we are examining now.

Monomania is almost always the first stage of a person's coming under the control of an ideology and a charismatic leader who is championing it, be it spiritual, political, or any other belief or doctrine. The victim will be interested in only books on one particular subject, watch video programs only about this topic, talk about nothing else and surround himself only with things related to this topic. It will be difficult to ignore. The victim may even quit watching news programs and any commercial programs that might conflict with the beliefs of the group so as to maintain purity of thought. The subjugator probably will demand this.

This goes far beyond common interest in a subject or a hobby; it can be literally debilitating. The mind and thought process becomes frozen in a pattern and will not deviate from it and any outside influence will be greatly discouraged by the grand manipulator. Everything else in that person's life will be viewed in reference to whatever this subject is and all else will have a fleeting importance to it. Monomania.

It is the first clear warning. And you can do something about it! It may be your one and only chance to put a halt to a process that if left unchecked will lead to the total domination of the victim by a subjugator. In ordinary cases, the victim will simply be overtaken by his own obsession with a topic and not be effected by an outside source. But in cult like situations – or any other environment in which other people are interested in a similar idea or project – there exists the serious danger of mind control.

There will be one person who is the foremost expert on this topic, who is considered infallible on the subject, and who is elevated to a godlike status by his followers. This is the person who will use his hypnotic influence over the victim and then expand that into brainwashing to provide himself with another devoted, mindless disciple. That is how it starts. A powerful, charismatic con man and a willing, usually innocent victim.

At this point you intervene, before the subjugator has a chance to overwhelm his victim. You hope you are already not too late. Timing of these matters is difficult. Since the victim had probably been attempting to keep secret her subjugation to the topic that has overcome her, the monomaniacal behavior may appear suddenly and without warning but already be in full development. But if not, you can act to stop further development between the victim and the looming subjugator.

The best strategy is to interact with the victim on the subject matter that is consuming most if not all of her time. Do not argue or debate over the topic. Discuss it intelligently and with interest. Then, gradually, interject alternative ideas and proposals concerning the topic that has overwhelmed her. This includes discussing any charismatic cult like personality who may be involved. Your purpose is not to attack the subject of interest or deride it but to offer other views that the victim may not be considering. Do not be an adversary. This will immediately turn you into an enemy and cause the victim to tenaciously defend her point of view and the looming subjugator's superiority.

The primary purpose is to break the pattern of fixation into which the victim has become locked, before she becomes entirely lost in it. It is also to determine how deeply she has become dominated by it. Beware, it may already be too late and the victim may already have decided that the subject has only one point from which it can be viewed and that the personality of note (subjugator) who is promoting it is infallible. If the victim claims something like the following about she and her leader: "Only he and I know what true reality is" she probably is beyond any reasonable reach...at the moment.

If more proof is needed that she is beyond reach and has succumbed to the will of the master and his rantings, listen for purely nonsensical comments that she may propound. Things which are in reality non defensible but which she will savagely defend anyway. This will give evidence that she has abandoned any attempt at critical thought ON THIS SUBJECT. Remember, she may still be able to form rational thoughts concerning other matters. But not this one. And this topic – whatever it may be – is the one that he or she has determined to be of the utmost importance and which overrides everything else.

This process must be interfered with at this point. If you have not been able to make any progress, possibly enlist the help of someone else whom the victim trusts and has relied on previously (or seek medical assistance). A former teacher, relative, minister – anyone who might cast a different light on the subject matter in question could help.

It is vital that the single-minded attachment the victim has placed on the debilitating topic be broken because it will lead to a much more dangerous condition: **Addiction**. The ideas to which the victim has become aligned with become embodied in the leader or director of the group or cult that represents these ideas and she will become addicted to him through them. He will represent everything she believes and trusts. The subjugator – if a male dominating a female – will masterfully impersonate the identity of the woman's father which will make the bond between them now incredibly difficult to break. Addiction to a person is almost like any other addiction. But they all share one cure: the only escape is abstinence from the object of addiction.

Trigger Controls

These are critical weapons of the subjugator's. They are usually words or phrases but can also be images and even scents, like certain fragrances of incense, perfume or cologne. Anything that can be tied to an emotion and an action associated with that emotion.

The subjugator wields exclusive power with these trigger controls. They are used to elicit a response by the victim and the triggers are known only to the subjugator. And they can be anything – a simple word like "Faster!" or the fragrance of sandalwood. The subjugator associates these with some form of atrocity that had been perpetrated on the victim which is revived in the fullness of terror later when the trigger control is activated.

In many cases, the trigger is a literal command, "You will obey me only!" This command can be relayed by any action performed by the subjugator such as the twirling of a neck chain he wears or even by stomping on the floor in a rhythmic way. When he performs one of these actions, the victim hears in the mind, "You will obey me only!" If a female, she may have first been introduced to these paired actions while suffering a beating at the hands of the subjugator or some other degrading assault. The trigger commands would likely be associated with some form of trauma. What they trigger is a severe emotional response based on that past trauma.

And these commands can be delivered in written form or by images. Particularly effective are voice mail messages which can be intended to shock the victim.

The triggers themselves are known only to the subjugator, as noted. The best way to uncover what they are is by reactions made by the victim during contact with the subjugator. If the victim's behavior suddenly changes it may be due to reading, hearing or even smelling a trigger command sent by the subjugator. The victim's reactions to any contact with the subjugator – any contact – must always be suspect and studied for clues to the content of the trigger commands.

Hypnosis vs. Brainwashing

As just noted above, almost anyone can perform hypnosis if the desire and the ability are available. Additionally, brainwashing is a procedure that also can be learned and performed by practically anyone with the proper training. Sometimes, a person even has the natural ability to perform these activities by the force of his own personality and will, like the famous monk Rasputin. Or for performing **Good Works** as in the great, Franz Anton Mesmer.

Hypnosis precedes brainwashing and then can be used in coordination with further mind control. Hypnosis is a relatively short-lived application to control a person's mind with limited power and over a limited time frame. It requires periodic refreshment of commands and, of great importance, it cannot be used to compel a person to act outside his own ethical and moral boundaries unless potent drugs are introduced and in this case control would still be questionable.

There are people who are immune to the effects of hypnosis – as most of us are aware – and this is compensated for by the subjugator by using drugs such as LSD and ketamine. Ketamine is particularly useful in breaking down a person's will. In cases such as those being examined in this book, the use of sophisticated drugs is very rare because the subjugator considers the victim's attachment to him as the most powerful of weapons and using drugs would serve to admit a need for assistance in controlling his victim. Also the type of highly sophisticated brainwashing drugs is far out of most person's ability to obtain.

Hypnosis opens the doorway into the subconscious and brainwashing creates the induced trauma that overwhelms the mind and soul.

Generally, hypnosis is used most forcefully and extensively at the beginning stages of mind control. It is through repeated and frequent mental suggestions that the victim will be emotionally separated from you. Like any other individuals, you and your loved one or friend have some matters of contention between you and other disagreements in regard to your outlook on life. The subjugator has stealthily learned about these from the victim and will take full advantage of any disagreements between the two of you and expand even minor problems into major differences by secretively implanting hypnotic suggestions in the victim's mind.

How specifically will this be accomplished? Step by step and point by point. An innuendo of your untrustworthiness and hostility will be placed in the victim's subconscious and increased in potency.

This can be done by way of phone calls, email, or any other form of contact had between the victim and the subjugator. Even small annoyances between you and the victim will be targeted. All of us have annoying mannerisms that bother our partner or friend. The subjugator will note this mannerism to the victim – innocently at first.

"Doesn't it sometimes annoy you the way John will sometimes grunt his answer to you?" the victim may be asked, knowing that this behavior bothers her. This behavior will sporadically be noted by the subjugator, like: "Is John still doing that disrespectful grunting?" Then the subjugator will increase the severity of the attack, like: "You know, John's grunting the way he does is really a sign of hostility." This may eventually develop into: "John must really hate you, doesn't he, treating you like that?"

This now causes the victim to consider the grunting as much more than a simple annoyance but as a serious insult and a true impediment to the relationship. At this point, the victim, will suddenly lash out at John when he responds to her with his usual grunt, "You make me sick the way you disrespect me with that grunting!" Often using the subjugator's own implanted wording.

John is taken aback. He was unaware how his grunting bothered his partner that much, or maybe that he was even doing it. Of course, grunting a reply is not the best way to communicate with another person, but it is a problem that can be logically discussed. But not now. It has been raised by the subjugator into a proof of hostility and maybe even hatred.

This is a **CRISIS POINT.** When the victim suddenly explodes with exaggerated rage over what normally is a minor annoyance or an insignificant problem that has existed between you. This has been elevated into a serious matter by the subjugator through his stealthily introduced hypnotic suggestions to the victim.

This type of animosity will be spread throughout all those living in the household. The purpose, of course, is to separate all inhabitants from the victim who then aligns himself staunchly with the subjugator.

The most compelling argument that the subjugator will use is that the dogma or ideology to which the victim and he adhere is more important than any outside relationship. Anyone who doesn't accept this ideology is the enemy, either because they are opposed to it, or they simply do not understand it.

"Spiritual" group leaders – sometimes called gurus – vigorously use this argument. They claim that their holy cause is more important than any relationships. They even warn the victim that most family members or friends will draw away from her because they cannot understand the true meaning of the ideology. And this helps develop the induced paranoia that the subjugator has been implanting in the victim with suggestions of deceit.

And, believing this is what's happening, the victim concludes that the reason she and her loved ones are arguing so much is because **THEY** are distancing themselves from her. The victim accepts the idea eventually that she should abandon family and other relationships and listen solely to the infallible leader and accept only his group.

At this point, the so-called "spirituality" cults and other ideologically strict societies insert a theory concerned with negative attachments to the world. This is a concept that is a major argument used to detach the victim from anyone and anything which has up until now been important in her life. Among these attachments which must be left behind are friends and family and all former ideas. By doing so, the victim will step onto the threshold of what is called "awakening" or, in other ideologies, self actualization, enlightenment, or simply – freedom. Freedom to become slave to the infallible master.

There is a blatantly self-serving contradiction with this philosophy. While the "novice" is expected to drop all attachments to the things of importance in his or her world, she is at the same time encouraged to become loyal to the ideologies of the group or cult and to pledge absolute fealty to its leader. While the leader of these groups will usually disparage marriage as an outmoded idea and will urge any married members to divorce his partner it is a different matter in regards to him. The master has the right to gather as many "wives" of any age as possible. Why so few people question this double-standard is a mystery since it is so obvious and blatant.

Ironically, in most cases, the charismatic leader of such groups is driven by a mania for sexual activity and happens to be endowed with an over-sized sexual apparatus and to possess the ability to maintain sexual activity for an abnormally lengthy duration. This seems to be an outgrowth of their other exaggerated psychotic characteristics.

The Assault on the Support Group

Your relationship with the victim – no matter what type it is – is under full scale attack and you probably do not even know it. You certainly don't know who's waging the attack. I will tell you who, and what you can do about it.

The attack is being waged by a charismatic leader – the head of the secret group, cult or closed organization – and he is doing it through the transmission of hypnotic suggestions through various sources, including Smartphone, laptop and even email and other forms of communication. He is quite creative in his assault. It is done by repeated derogatory and negative comments about you with each contact. What is being instilled is distrust and paranoia. It is possible for the subjugator to accomplish this because he has the trust of the victim who believes in the same things as he does – at least the victim believes so.

The victim has been told and accepts that she and the subjugator exist on a higher level than you and others of her former support group and that you are jealous of both of them. She believes that you are attempting to separate the two of them (daughter from father, or are they now two lovers?) and the victim must prevent this at all costs. Note how now she has more in common with the subjugator than she does with you and that you and the victim are basically enemies at this point.

And that is a primary clue which reveals the validity of the existence of mind control. Do you feel like the enemy now? You are the enemy of the victim, your friend or loved one? Why do you feel that way? What made you enemies?

When the subjugator is communicating with the victim, the words he is using aren't just simple remarks but because they are being spoken to a person who is under hypnotic influence they carry the weight of pronouncements. You the defender aren't just "listless" in your attentiveness to your friend or loved one, but "abandoning" toward him or her. You aren't just "casual" in the way you raise money for living expenses, but you are "lazy," maybe even to the point of being a "moocher." These are the ideas being placed in your friend or loved one's mind and solidified by seemingly innocuous trigger words such as "listless and casual."

Using hypnotic suggestions has the advantage of doing the most psychological damage because they are being implanted in the subconscious. However, this form of control has one MAJOR disadvantage. The commands – trigger words which empower the negative images – must be refreshed approximately every 3rd day. They begin to fade in power after 2 days and quickly dissipate in strength after 3. At the 3 day mark, the negative images lose strength. This means that the subjugator must keep in relatively constant contact with the victim in order to maintain a strong level of control.

Your strategy at this point is obviously to keep the subjugator from contacting the victim as much as you can. This may be extremely difficult since you may not always know when the 2 are communicating, since triggers can be relayed through writing – such as text messages – although they will not have as much potency when delivered in this form. But the commands can be left as voice messages on telephone systems. These are quite potent. It will be almost impossible for you to monitor these.

You will know when the subjugator and the victim HAVE NOT been in contact for 3 or more days. Your friend or lover's behavior will be noticeably different. She or he will be decidedly less hostile to you. It is really remarkable how this change of behavior occurs surely and like clockwork. Like everything else I am relating on this entire topic, I have experienced this effect of lack of contact between the subjugator and victim. It is particularly depressing when they resume contact because the negative effect is immediately noticeable; the subjugator's control is that clearly defined.

And the form of that resumed contact may be a simple voice message on an Smartphone. Just hearing his voice. Or even a text message which hits powerful "trigger" words in its wording will strike the victim's subconscious.

You may bring this observation of changed behavior to the attention of the victim. He or she may even notice it and begin to have suspicions about the subjugator instead of suspicions about you. Of course, the reverse can happen and the victim can see this as an attempt by you to conspire against she and the subjugator. But it is time for you to take that chance. Time is running out. Your friend or loved one is on the verge of departing. What have you got to lose at this point?

Your friend or loved one has become fixated on a particular topic and has begun treating you with disrespect and hatred. You will probably try to convince yourself that this behavior is only temporary and will run its course. Do not fall into this trap! Do not convince yourself that it will get better or that she will return to normal soon. **This will not happen.** You must act to change the situation if you still can.

The victim will assail you with rigid arguments, most of which are designed by the subjugator. It will be futile to argue them because only the subjugator has the acceptable response. However, there is one argument that may be used against you which is so patently absurd that you may be able to make a nick in it with a counter argument and cause at least some daylight of original thought.

You will probably hear an argument like the following one which is the basic propaganda message created to finally separate the victim from you and everyone in his support group. This is what the victim will tell you: "Me and the others in the group were warned that you, my friends, and even my family, wouldn't be able to understand us and that you would pull away from us and try to fight us. Losing friends and family members to the cause (or beliefs) is something we have to expect and to accept if we want to continue to follow the path (whatever that path may be). And, since **<u>our beliefs are far more important than any personal ties</u>**, and you are against us anyway, I will have to leave you behind and join my new family." The underlined above is the classic ultimate argument almost all such groups use and implant into their victim's minds. Be on guard when you hear it!

While I generally do not suggest arguing any points with the victim since logic is no longer being accepted by her or him, in this case I do suggest asking a question like the following: "Since your beliefs are supposed to be beneficial to everyone – even me and the other people you know – how is it beneficial to society if you turn your back on the very basics on which all of society is based : the stability of friend and family no matter what belief system any of us follow? How is that a good thing?"

Don't expect an honest response to that. The true reason for asking it is that it will hopefully plant a seed in the subconscious of the victim which gradually will mature into the question: "Well, what does society truly gain by making my friends and family my enemy, even should I join a higher group?" Yes, a type of brainwashing, but I feel allowed in this one case because it could destroy over time the basic philosophy of hate and discord with which the victim is being immersed without his or her true consent.

If you have come to this point, the situation is dire and emergency action is needed. And a literal emergency is what may have to occur to break your friend or loved one free from this powerful domination. Something which will be of such consequence that it will shock your friend or loved one back into reality, but something not harmful to anyone. Otherwise, your friend or loved one is lost and what follows is what most likely will take place just before he or she leaves.

Weapon of Silence

One of the best ways to develop animosity between two people is for both people to quit speaking to each other. It will make 2 people enemies quickly. Even the simple barrier of silence itself creates an animosity on its own. The subjugator is keenly aware of this and knows how to create this wall of silence between the victim and those in the support group.

First, the victim and her partner (friend) must be made to bicker incessantly, fostering increasing periods of silence between them simply to avoid the negativity. This will lead to an eventual total breakdown of communication.

Bickering can be instigated by administering hypnotic suggestions to the victim. Remember, these suggestions need not be elaborate; they may literally be just derogatory suggestions made about her "friend or loved one" and are in some fashion delivered to the victim – by text message, phone (direct or messaging), email, in person, or etc.

The loss of communication is another **CRISIS POINT**. There is another method, an ingenious method beside hypnotic suggestion used to instigate this loss of communication, that was employed by one of the fake "gurus" who was mentioned earlier. He commanded the victim to tell her partner or friend that it is important for her (victim) to embark upon an INDEFINITE period of self-induced silence. Theoretically, for the purpose of gaining control of her thoughts and for entering into a more meditative state. What this in reality does is shut down all communication INDEFINITELY between the victim and any available support group. Obviously, the term indefinitely is of extreme importance. How long is indefinitely?

This declined form of verbal contact will also heighten hostilities and confirm the idea in the victim's mind – implanted by the subjugator – that there is a serious problem in her relationship with her partner or friend. No matter the true state of affairs. They aren't speaking to each other any longer, are they? Of course there's a problem between them. And at this point, there **IS** a problem between them, but an artificially produced one.

The **ultimate** goal of the subjugator in all of these preliminary machinations is to gain physical control over the victim. Once this is accomplished, actual brainwashing can begin – not necessarily the highly complex and sophisticated technical type that might be performed by the CIA or other organizations but a basic form of mind control that will nonetheless produce the same type of results.

Once communication with the support group is short circuited, the next stage in the process is usually physical separation of the victim from the people that make up this group. Separation from the support group is another **CRISIS POINT.** And it may be the most significant crisis point because once the victim is out of reach of the support group, he becomes almost totally under control of the subjugator. Inasmuch as it is such a drastic measure, it is usually performed secretly – the victim simply departs without warning. If this occurs and all contact is lost, there is little hope of re-establishing relations with the victim short of employing a private detective.

Once the victim has departed from home, the situation becomes immediately desperate. But if the victim is still uncertain about leaving, one other way that could be used to convince her to leave and which will surely destroy any relationships with the support group is by cyber attack arranged by the subjugator.

Hacking a Relationship

If the wall of silence, the incessant bickering and the insinuations of untrustworthiness have not yet destroyed the relationship between the victim and you and her support group, there is another weapon that can be used which might level the fatal blow. A personalized cyber assault. It is usually at this juncture in the overall attack that it is used. And it can be DEVASTATING!

The subjugator probably operates a website and uses various other technical methods for contacting his followers, no matter the type of organization. He will also employ at least one person who is in control of the entire cyber network and is an expert, almost certainly a master hacker. This is a mighty weapon.

CRISIS POINT. A personalized attack will be waged on the victim's support group and you and, unless the ones assaulted by it can counter it, they will most likely be made to appear as hateful, conspiring, enemies. Few people will be able to counter the attack; most will not even know how it occurred or even that it occurred. The victims of these attacks (you and the others in the support group) would need to be either master cyber hackers themselves or have access to a person of such abilities to be able to withstand the massive damage that will be inflicted.

This is how the attack takes place. Tapping into your own cyber system – computer, Smartphone, etc. – the hacker, who is working under directions of the subjugator, will send a hateful, vicious message about the **victim** (person you are trying to save) apparently from you to another member of the victim's support group. But instead of being delivered to any of them, the message will be sent to the **victim** (the person you are trying to save). She will see this as a conspiratorial, disparaging message which she believes has been MISTAKENLY sent to her by you. Not only will this message be painful in content to the victim – probably including some form of negative sexual content – but it will solidify her belief in your complete untrustworthiness and cause her to accept without question all of the negative things that the subjugator has been broadcasting about you for weeks.

The key to the attack is that the insulting message will appear to have been sent directly from one of your devices and will have all of the identifying features associated with your system. If the victim even reveals her receipt of this to you there is seemingly not any argument you can make as a defense that he or she would accept. No one else could have sent that horrible message from your device but you – right?

You could try arguing that someone broke into your cyber nerwork and sent this damning message instead of you. But the hacker that was employed by the subjugator even accounts for this argument. He arranges the hacking to be done at a time and from a location which pinpoints you and only you at the place and the time that the message was sent from the particular offending device.

Devious and devastating. And this is if you were "lucky" enough to have been informed of receipt of the damning message by the victim. Often, the victim will be so incensed that he or she will not even tell the would-be defender about this lethal message and flee into the arms and the world of the subjugator without announcement.

This is not fiction. I experienced a cyber assault of exactly this nature which caused a furious response that is beyond description.

I was lucky. I had access to a hacker myself associated with an unnamed intelligence agency. By observing all elements of my system, he was able to warn me of the impending cyber attack by backtracking down a source that had been monitoring my system as well as monitoring the victim's system. I knew it was coming but only approximately when but I couldn't stop it. However, I could after the fact explain to the victim how it had been done. Unfortunately, most people will not have access to their own expert hacker like I did.

There is one potential defense you could use. Note if any other people in your network had also been hacked at the same time. For some reason – maybe ego – the cyber hacker isn't usually content with only hacking you, but others who are on your system. And this is a powerful clue. Demonstrating that others were hacked at the same time is proof you can use.

Unless you have the ready defenses that I had, a specifically directed cyber attack can take place and will most likely cause the victim to depart in haste into the world of the subjugator. And – by this point – after all of the hostilities you have experienced, the subjugator expects that you might greet the victim's departure with a relieved, "Good riddance!"

Before giving up on the victim, remind yourself that he or she truly is a victim and is working under the control of another person who is the true **enemy!**

Other Causes of Departure

Often, the subjugator uses a less dramatic means of bringing about the departure of his victim from his or her support group and/or home. The subjugator is by nature a bully and a coward and wants as little resistance as possible from all parties concerned. But, remember, he is also usually of genius intellect and can devise some very imaginative and compelling scenarios by which to remove the victim from her support group without causing too much alarm

One of these is connected to and an extension of the self-imposed silence that the victim placed upon herself – upon the order of the subjugator supposedly for peace and meditative purposes. In preparation for her departure, the victim announces an upcoming "silent retreat" that she plans to attend in some relatively distant location (a couple - to several hundred miles distant) with a group of like minded searchers.

The "retreat" is sponsored by the subjugator. For your information – THERE REALLY IS NO "RETREAT."

This "retreat" ploy is used if the victim is involved in a "spiritual' type of group. Another type of group will sponsor a different type of gathering, be it a UFO abductees reunion or New World Order update symposium or maybe Fourth Reich Seminar. Each will have some type of initiation meeting which the victim can attend with the least amount of interference from his or her support group. The meeting is meant to sound non-threatening to outside observers.

These "meetings" are supposed to be similar to common seminars or class reunions or even lodge gatherings. They seem non-threatening and plausible. This would be true **IF YOU WERE BEING TOLD THE TRUTH.**

There is another ingenious method that the subjugator uses to extract his victim from his support group with the least resistance from anyone – health reasons. The subjugator claims that he needs the victim to come to his aid for a short period due to a health condition of an obscure nature. It is his practice to require his followers or those who are new to the group or sect or cult to assist him in day-to-day clerical, organizational activities because of a health condition that is never specifically detailed. And, of course, he claims there will be several people in attendance (which is probably a lie). The subjugator wants to get the victim alone for personal indoctrination which usually includes sex.

Thus, as a sign of concern for the leader and as a show of support for the group and its ideals, the victim agrees to go to his aid for an unspecified amount of time and often with the defender's – your – skeptical approval. Such is the clever trap that is laid by the subjugator.

How can there be any harm in aiding an ailing person especially when other people will also be there to help? That's an act of mercy, isn't it? Also, since the subjugator claims to be in poor health it is highly unlikely that he will be a physical – and/or sexual threat – to the victim. (There will be a great deal more to add to the idea of the leader's "declining health" later).

So, if the victim hasn't simply vacated without warning, she may leave under the seemingly logical conditions just noted. But beware, at this point, most if not all of the scant information that the victim has supplied about this "innocent" trip, for whatever claimed, purpose will be a lie. But a lie that is expertly concealed by the people who are in charge of organizing this "meeting" or other reason given for the visit. And additionally a lie with which the victim is in full cooperation. This person whom you used to trust can no longer be trusted. **You MUST understand and ACCEPT this!** And, ironically, if you question any of these proposals you will be accused of distrust and trying to spy on the victim.

Another reason the victim may leave to join the subjugator is that the victim is in love with him or believes that her love for the manipulator is genuine. Emotional attraction must be considered as a reason for departure – real or imagined by the victim.

Gone

Gone! A person you deeply cared about is no longer there. The feeling is, as they say, palpable. You can feel it. All of a sudden it is as if you are at the bottom of a well looking upward and nobody is there. At least, that was how I would describe how I felt about the void that was left when the person I cared about so deeply was really...gone. And you are left wondering – WHAT HAS JUST HAPPENED? Lost in bewilderment and confusion with no starting point at which to reach for a solution.

The removal happened either without any warning or with your knowledge but with limited information. And of this information, little if any of it can trusted as being reliable. Even the emergency phone number you were given by the victim as a contact person is probably useless.

Now what!

All communication between the victim and you and any others of the former support group will probably cease. Nothing. Not a word or a message of any kind, despite all of the promises that the "departed" would keep in regular contact.

You try contacting the emergency number you were given. There is never an answer but possibly there is a recorded message. You never receive a return answer.

Maybe your friend or loved one was kidnapped or is being held against his or her will in the more conventional sense. He already has been victimized in the mind control sense.

What else can you do but call the police? Because the given location of the victim's destination may be a hundred or more miles distant, a blind trip there would be foolhardy. The call to the police is of no use. You are told that if the victim is over the age of 18 and in sound mental condition that he can go anywhere he wants for any length of time he wants without reporting to anyone.

You try asking the police to at least try a wellness visit to the address that the victim gave you. This will probably produce no results.

Will the victim ever return? That depends on the type of organization or cult into which he or she has become indoctrinated. Sometimes the victim remains at the ashram, campus, compound – or whatever type of central facility the group maintains – for an indefinite period. This generally means that they will remain there as long as their services are required by the leader and they are of use.

Consider this: a person is usually brainwashed in order to later be released into public and spread the doctrines of the group and worship of its leader. They are not brainwashed in order to remain behind and keep these "great" secrets hidden in the compound, ashram, complex, or whatever the headquarters is called. There are only 2 reasons for rejecting a member, old age and poor health, which is a quality to be determined on arrival for indoctrination.

The victim probably will return home at some point after both brainwashing and indoctrination have been accomplished. This is when deprogramming can be attempted not while the victim is in custody. Often, however, when the victim returns "home" this is only a period of increased hostility. She isn't "home" to be deprogrammed, but to carry out the master's instructions and even to try to convert or destroy you.

Keep in mind the following: if the victim does not truly love her subjugator, she is surely addicted to him and almost all addicts subconsciously hate their addiction and would like to escape. You will provide the escape route.

How to determine if the victim truly loves her subjugator? The only way to answer that is in the results of the deprogramming. If it's true love, she will freely choose to accept all of his lies and abuses and will not be torn from him. But if the love is an illusion implanted in her mind, the exposing of the techniques of brainwashing will make that "love" just as fake.

You must warn yourself that the victim may truly be in love with the subjugator. Is it your right to control who the victim loves or doesn't love? It's a question I seriously had to ask myself.

Forcing a Response

The victim has departed home and has not been heard from for over 2 weeks. There may have been some scantily devised text messages of one form or another which may not even have been sent by the victim. All verbal contact has been denied. Nothing is known of her or her whereabouts.

All of the contact numbers that the victim had given before departure have been tried but are either fraudulent or useless. The police of the municipality to which the victim has theoretically gone refused assistance. The problem you are faced with is how to force a person to make contact with you when that person does not wish to do so or possibly because her "captor" has forbidden her to do so. You are relatively sure of her safety because you believe it was she who has sent a few lines of text of limited detail only to let you know she is still alive somewhere.

(The activities I took were successful for me. No one can guarantee the outcome when used in any other situation).

ACTION TAKEN: At this point, I knew that extreme measures are to be used because all else has failed. A powerful and extremely forceful message is sent to the victim by email or the surest form to reach the intended recipient. This message is **NOT** to be sent by anyone who has already previously attempted contact, regardless of proposed content.

The message is to be sent by an interested "third party" who knows the victim and is closely associated with members of her family and/or support group. It could be a relative or even a spouse of a child of the victim's. The primary requirement is that this person has not yet tried to contact the victim and that he is well acquainted with the victim in one way or another.

CONTENT OF THE MESSAGE: It must be severe and strike directly at the inhumane way in which the victim is treating friends and loved ones. It must not use euphemisms – mild alternative descriptions – but clear, exact, shocking language in order to get the full attention of the victim (and subjugator). The message must begin powerfully and without apology. An example is below:

We've been trying to contact you for some time but in your self-centered concern only for your conceited self you have refused to reply. Obviously you have no feeling for those who you used to love or called friends otherwise you wouldn't have cut us off from all contact with the same lack of caring a child abuser has for his victim. Is that the higher understanding that this new belief of yours has taught you? Maybe yours isn't such a lofty path? To deny even the simplest response is cruel and sadistic especially to those who are closest to you and love you most (name daughters, sons, etc). If this is who the new you is then maybe it's best you never contact any of us again. Disgust is all I feel for you now. I hope your new friends don't find out what kind of cheat and liar you really are. Or maybe that's why they like you.

Pretty strong stuff, as the idiom goes. But it has to be. The purpose is to get a verbal response, not any particular response – just any reply beyond the simple scratching of pointless texts that may have been offered earlier. It is the hope that the victim will be shocked by this message into understanding the damage his actions have caused. But it can only be used once! **Only once!**

Remember who the real enemy is. This ultimatum for a reply puts him on notice that people who are concerned are watching. And if something untoward should happen to the victim there will be consequences. Being that he is a bully and a coward, this will get his attention. And, be sure, the victim is always under close surveillance and any communication he receives will be read or heard or seen by the subjugator.

WHAT TO DO IF THERE IS STILL NO RESPONSE?

Make one final contact attempt with the victim, stating that your next action will be a **911** call (or whatever is used for emergencies in that location) because you think a kidnapping of the victim has occurred. Just making the threat may get a response.

If you do not hear any response you should prepare yourself for the possibility that the victim has been lost. He or she may actually want to be controlled by the subjugator and to devote all energies to his welfare and greatness. You may have to accept this. Deprogramming can only succeed on a person who wants this help – even if only subconsciously at the moment – and one who is no longer under the physical control of her subjugator.

IN PERSON ASSAULT

The subjugation of the will of one person to another person usually starts with the first contact and may seem a completely innocent occurrence. The subjugator generally has his victim targeted from the moment the two meet, be it in person, online or in any other fashion that two human beings make conscious contact. They are first drawn together by seemingly sharing a specific ideology, almost always concerning the object of the victim's obsessive behavior. The subjugator usually uses this ideology as a scam to capture his victims rather than having a deep belief in it as already noted.

A mild form of hypnosis is usually introduced at the earliest opportunity to control the victim. This sets the stage for deeper mind control later. A person does not have to be an expert or a physician to perform basic hypnosis and may not even know he is using hypnosis if he is already adept at beguiling people. A victim does not have to go under a trance to be hypnotized. Ever been hypnotized behind the driver's steering wheel?

Some people have a natural ability to hypnotize others. It's a relatively simple procedure that can be introduced on a computer monitor, smartphone screen or over any other form of visual communication as well as in person, of course. Later, verbal commands will be the only contact needed to refresh the implanted orders and these commands can be delivered in various fashion but only by the one who placed them.

CRISIS POINT. Hypnosis is powerful, yet it can be introduced quickly and without anyone's notice since, as noted, the victim need not come under a true trance. It can be performed by a person whom the victim believes trustworthy. The subjugator approaches the distraught person, reaches out his hand in friendship and says in a monotone voice something like: "Hello, I can see that you are troubled. I am here to help you. You can trust me. Tell me what I can do for you."

Sound too simple? The above act when properly performed by a person skilled in the art of deception (a con man) can be devastatingly effective when wielded against someone who is trusting and perhaps experiencing personal difficulties at the time. This prepares the way for later incursions into the victim's mind, and is the first act that opens it to penetration. As simple as that!!

An even more detailed example will next be illustrated to reveal added elements of a hypnotic assault on a person. Picture the above scenario about the trustworthy appearing person (subjugator) offering his assistance to a vulnerable person. Suppose, at the instance of meeting between he and his victim – before a word is spoken – the manipulator makes a very slight misstep to the left when approaching his victim. Reaching out his hand to shake hers, he awkwardly bumps into her. The handshake still took place but maybe amid embarrassed smiles.

This planned clumsiness is **VERY** important. It immediately places the intended victim off balance both physically and psychologically. Something is very slightly amiss, noticeable but seemingly accidental and trivial. This maneuver makes the victim off guard and as such unprepared and leaves the mental processes off balance. Further, it shifts all control to the subjugator.

If there were someone there – a friend of the victim – to intervene at this point, a different outcome than his subjugation could most likely result.

The people who exercise mind control are brilliantly devious and adept. But methods that are equally brilliant and effective have been developed to counter them. One of the most important weapons is knowledge of the devices being used by the subjugator to overcome a victim. When the trick is uncovered it loses its power. But this realization usually occurs after initial damage has been done.

The victim cannot be expected to know beforehand of the planned off-balance maneuver perpetrated by the subjugator or the hypnotic artifice involved. **But understanding later what happened and how it affected the victim is critical when unraveling the layers of behavior modification which were used to bring the victim under control.**

Replaying the first actions used to apply control to the victim is undeniable evidence to the victim that brainwashing did occur. The recovering victim will find it difficult to argue that such an event did not happen when specifics involved in the activity of brainwashing are demonstrated. **REPEATING: This is a vital part of recovery – peeling away the tactics of mind control so that the victim can see the mental devices that were used to overcome him. REVEAL THE TRICK!**

Not only will the trick be revealed, but so too the character of the person who performed it. Is the subjugator such a weak person that he needs to trick someone into following his suggestions or advice or to like him as a person? The victim must come to ask this himself.

The beginning of subjugation to another person has many scenarios. But the process is basically the same in all of them, as just laid out. The victim is targeted, an awkward situation occurs, the victim is given the initial hypnotic suggestion (whether or not the offender knows he is using hypnosis) and the victim begins to succumb to his doctrine, no matter the subject, be it religious, political or other.

But the doctrine or ideology is only a tool for the con man. He uses it to aggrandize himself and in most instances as a way to enrich himself. Himself and no one else. Unfortunately, the victim may accept as sacred the ideology that the subjugator is using for his scam. This not only destroys her faith in something that may be positive, but gives the subjugator a great deal more power and authority over the victim.

The Brainwashing Suite

As you may recall, several stages occur during the process of mind control. The first, and perhaps most critical stage, is separating the victim from his or her support group. A great deal of effort and time is spent on this. This is because once the victim no longer has any other outside contact with reality other than the subjugator's the victim's mind and world can now be molded to the captor's desire. This is accomplished through brainwashing. Hypnosis was used to lead the victim to this point. While hypnosis alone cannot alter the worldview of the victim; brainwashing can.

Brainwashing is a methodical process that does not have to rely upon highly technical equipment and drugs as is so frequently depicted on television or the movies. That is far beyond the sophistication and ability of the type of mind controlling groups with which we are dealing. But the results that are produced by the groups under consideration are very similar and the victim can be deeply controlled.

Once the victim is physically detached from a support group, the brainwashing begins. Even though the victim is not usually restrained in any way or imprisoned, there is the sense of confinement in that the victim is housed at a specified location and has limited access to communication and transportation. This represents a form of confinement because the subconscious is aware that there are some forms of low level physical constraint being maintained.

After a brief "honeymoon" period with the group, the victim will be subjected to lengthy one-on-one sessions with the group's charismatic leader who will torture her with hours of dogma. This will be sandwiched between periods of sleep deprivation and lengthening hours of enforced hunger. This naturally breaks down the will.

Some "spiritual gurus" claim that this is actually breaking down the EGO. This is a concept that the victim can accept which is why she does accept it. And, if the group is some form of rigid, secret society, the victim is told that these hardships make him or her a more powerful defender of the "cause." But in reality, these tactics are meant to break down the WILL – which is not the same as the EGO – with the purpose of making him a devoted follower of the leader.

The will is one's ability to make rational decisions for oneself and to determine what reality is. The EGO is the inner force which usually causes conflict in the individual by presenting negative narratives concerning life situations. AT least, that is one term for the EGO and I believe it is one of the best. But no matter how you describe it, the EGO is different from the will. And in any venue breaking down a person's will is a negative, highly destructive procedure.

Next, the victim will be forced to perform menial, degrading tasks. Theoretically, this is for the purpose of teaching him humility and the necessity of obedience to a person of higher standing. What it in fact does is take away what remains of the victim's self esteem and establishes the head of the group as someone whose superiority is beyond questioning.

The menial tasks that the victim must perform are similar to common activities, but they are made degrading in nature. For example, the victim may be assigned to clean the floor but while in the process of cleaning the floor other members of the group may soil the floor directly in front of her and make the process of removing the debris or stains much more difficult by grinding the filth into the floor or smashing it in a messy heap, etc. This same strategy will be applied to any other basic chore such as cleaning the bathroom, serving dinner or making beds.

Some "chores" will be a particularly debasing form of sexual deviancy or acts forcing the victim to contact other members private parts in ways that are personally disgusting to him. This is most common, oddly enough, in so-called "spiritual" groups. You will recall that the leaders of these groups, fashioning themselves as "gurus," usually have an excessively overdeveloped sexual capacity. Attending to this need is one of the demands made on the devotees.

By this time, the victim may have already become addicted to the charismatic leader. She may also consider his demand for sexual contact as a benefit or a favor to her because it is one of the foul beliefs of many of these sects that the "guru" has the power of god within him and that he transmits this to his followers through physical sex in ritual intercourse called skaktipat. This includes even married women. To this point, I must note that the woman who agrees to have this type of sexual encounter may not be responsible for her actions any longer. While basic hypnosis cannot force one to go beyond his moral boundaries, there aren't any boundaries that brainwashing cannot break through.

Brainwashing is so powerful because it is administered during times of trauma and deep distress to produce an indelible effect on the mind. Every part of the victim's life comes under the control of the master and most forms of privacy are violated, even the act of using the washroom for necessary bodily functions and cleansing are kept under observation.

Pledge of Guilt

One of the first requirements that will be demanded of the victim is an unspoken pledge of fealty (guilt). I call it a pledge of guilt because this will be the primary weapon that the subjugator will use to keep the victim firmly and ruthlessly bound. The victim may not even be aware of this, but guilt will be one of the emotions that prevents escape from the tormentor. Guilt!

But, why guilt? What should the victim feel guilty about? Through his hypnotic suggestions, the subjugator has convinced the victim that he has done many great things for him and that it is a special privilege to be among his followers (no matter the group or organization). This makes the victim feel obliged to remain true and devoted to the subjugator and to not even consider straying outside his influence or entertain any conflicting ideas or beliefs. This sense of indebtedness only strengthens the addiction to the subjugator. But keep this in mind: one emotion common to most addicts is a hatred for the drug which keeps them imprisoned.

Many of the subjugators also use deteriorating health as a way of maintaining the fidelity of their followers. While pretending to be powerful both in mind and body, the subjugators often complain of a mysterious underlying illness which it is understood is slowly, gradually killing them. But they claim to be sustaining themselves through it with great strength and perseverance. They seem to be experiencing a never ending death.

The victim is forced to be ever attentive to this condition – which in reality does not exist – and is made to feel guilty if not concerned every moment for the master's health and safety. I knew of one person who maintained a constant, daily vigil on the life of his subjugator and kept an almost hourly contact with him.

This can be a critical element in brainwashing once a victim is addicted to his subjugator. And it was one of the most difficult and confounding scenarios I faced while actively deprogramming. One of the subjugators was described by his victim as a highly attractive, sexual dynamo, immensely strong and powerful who at the same time was also covered with lesions and infected with a mysterious disease that was killing him for which he was under continual treatment. It was impossible to reconcile these 2 descriptions of one man.

What made it even more difficult to explain is that the subjugator kept appointments with specialists and the physical results that were obtained showed he suffered from serious conditions. Yet it was claimed by more than one source that he was still a powerful, sexually vigorous person even though the condition that was supposedly killing him was debilitating! How could this possibly be?

All of the other delusions created by this con man had been demystified except the secret of how he produced the illusion of unbounded health and vigor while on the constant verge of dying. It was the last of his tricks to finally be exposed, and it was an amazing con because it required a person of extraordinary ability and mental defectiveness to perform.

The astonishing fact wasn't just that he could fake the illness to perfection but, as noted, physical test results of an undeniable nature testified to his deteriorating condition. X-rays. Ultrasounds, etc.. Physical evidence – and not delusions planted in the minds of the doctors – that he was dying. How!!

The answer was discovered by accident, while studying outdated medical books. A now unused term for a medical/metaphysical condition known as *pseudologia fantastica* came to attention. A more common name for this condition is pathological lying. However, among its suborders of traits is a condition known as mythomania. This is when a person creates a life history of himself which is fictional but which he believes with such a force of power that he endows it with reality. On occasion a person with this condition creates an illness as part of his life which he convinces others really exists.

This isn't just a matter of a person being able to perfectly fake an illness, it's a matter where he can affect the physical outcome of medical tests through his own will or mental powers. Of course, it is an exceptionally rare ability often requiring a high genius intellect to accomplish. Not ironically, it is always associated with a maniacally narcissistic personality type.

At any rate, one of the cult leaders with whom I sparred possessed this extremely rare condition. It is highly unlikely you will be faced with a person with his abilities but I note him for completeness.

Sex is Control

The victim will probably engage in intimate sexual relations with the subjugator, and most likely this will happen among the so-called "spiritual" cults or groups dealing with philosophical beliefs as opposed to other organizations which also use brainwashing to recruit and keep its followers. Sex will be used primarily for control rather than enjoyment by the group leader. You may have to accept the idea that your friend or loved one has had consensual sex – maybe frequently – with the subjugator. At best it can be explained as occurring under duress. At worst, the sex act is little more than non-violent rape.

Sex is a powerful tool of control and subjugation. Not only does it force two people together in a raw, physical act but it often suggests the existence of a strict domination of the male over the female.

During the sex act "trigger" words or commands are ingrained into the victim's subconscious. In any form, the act of sex is a physically strenuous, forceful eruption of passion, no matter the true emotion felt on either side. Words of a non-romantic nature will be spoken or even shouted out as the bodies are thrusting together in "lovemaking." The purpose is to create a "trigger" that can be used at a later time to exactly reproduce the intensity of the moment and recreate the identical feelings of helplessness, shame – or guilty elation in the victim.

The words that are used can be a simple command like: "Faster! Smile. Do it right. This is a waste of time!" And these will be paired with whatever subconscious trauma that the subjugator wants his victim to experience when he shouts these commands (or later writes them in a text or etc.).

This is a very powerful way to control the mind and is almost impossible to neutralize because only the subjugator knows what the trigger words are. The feelings that are supposed to be aroused are ones of terror, panic, dread, guilt and paranoia. The words activate the traumatic response. The only real way to prevent the activation of these commands is to avoid all contact with the subjugator.

The victim's sexual activity with the subjugator may be the most painful aspect of brainwashing that it will be difficult if not impossible for you to ignore or withstand. Remind yourself that she is a victim and that no one has the right to control another person's mind. Also beware, when you ask the victim directly if sexual activity was part of the relationship with the subjugator she will almost certainly lie and say, "No." That has been my experience in 100 % of the cases with which I have dealt. Expect not to be told the truth.

A Sound Torture

Another extremely powerful method of mind control is exercised through the use of sound and music. It is a technique that has been used for many centuries. In classical types of music, certain pieces are written using a diminished 5th or augmented 4rth tritone which means that they are out of the ordinary octave and result in a disharmonious tune that is aggravating to the subconscious of most listeners. It is meant to be annoying, unnerving and, in some instances, maddening. This is a well known ploy in musical composition whose intent is to disorient and confuse the listener and is sometimes referred to as the "Devil's tritone."

While this type of warping of the musical scale is not typically used in modern day brainwashing, it is a form of in-harmonics that can add to the effects of other sonic measures used to attack the will. A much more commonly used and modern form of musical attack is the subliminal implanting of direct commands beneath a melody. There is a skill to this travesty of music that can be as highly developed as that required to play concert piano.

Subliminal hypnotic commands are hidden beneath the melody of the music. This will have a devastating effect on the unsuspecting listener. While the conscious mind is totally absorbed by the melody, the underlying subliminal verbal commands become ingrained into the subconscious just as the musical notes are ingrained into the grooves of vinyl records. Of course, today, magnetic tape, digital recording systems and even more sophisticated methods are used; but they are no less powerful at brainwashing than the words hidden beneath vinyl recordings.

It is possible for someone to acquire the sophisticated equipment needed to underlay a voice beneath a recording. The head of a cult or other organization would surely see the importance of such an investment.

It would only require the subjugator to record whatever commands he wishes to implant into the subconscious of the victim on some form of recording device and then place the melody from that person's favorite song or songs over the commands. It is important that the subjugator's voice is used, however, even though it will not be immediately audible to the listener. The victim's subconscious will recognize it.

It works this way. The subconscious mind operates at a speed of hearing at about 1,200 to 1,400 words per minute. The conscious mind hears about 250 to 450 words per minute. A hypnotic script is read at conversational speed (250 – 450) words per minute into a recording device which then speeds these words up to subconscious hearing levels of 1,200 to 1,400 words per minute. (NSA statistics). When this sped up script is placed beneath music which is played at a normal speed the words of the script can be heard by the subconscious mind but not heard by the conscious ear. And the impact on the person listening to the script is ravaging to the psyche.

"You passionately love only me and will become uncontrollably jealous over anyone trying to gain my affections." "Only I can make your life whole and you must pledge absolute obedience to me." "You cannot trust anyone else in your life because they are our enemies." "You and I are one unit and to act against me in any way is the worst of all betrayals and will destroy your very soul."

Above are 4 powerful commands. They were chosen to be highlighted because they are among the most devastating that can be given and they are the most common type for that reason.

In the first one, the victim is convinced that she loves the subjugator. Can he really force her into truly loving him through brainwashing? Only if she wants to be so influenced. This is similar to hypnosis. But in brainwashing, she can be convinced that she BELIEVES she loves this person which in most instances is a strong enough control to keep the victim emotionally dependent on him. This "spell" can be broken but only with extreme difficulty.

The second command that was given is also critical and a common one that is forced upon the victim. "Only I can make your life whole and you must pledge absolute obedience to me." I refer to this as a Pledge of Guilt. What this command ultimately does is encloses the victim in a netting of guilt which tightens around him anytime he should ever stray from protecting the subjugator or attempts engaging in freedom of thought beyond what he is told to think. And if such should happen, the victim is not worthy of all of those benefits which the master has supposedly provided for him in making his life whole.

The third command makes sure that the victim will not stray to any other belief system or be influenced by any other person than the subjugator. "You cannot trust anyone else in your life because they are our enemies."

The fourth commandment: "You and I are one unit and to act against me in any way is the worst of all betrayals and will destroy your very soul." This makes it impossible for the victim to find any fault with the subjugator and to support him in any and all matters

Imagine these 4 commands assaulting the victim's subconscious, arising from beneath the tones of her favorite music! Repeatedly.

And if the subjugator plays a musical instrument and has a passable singing voice, he could craft some particularly meaningful lyrics with which to subdue his victim. Lyrics possess a special quality for tampering with the psychic pattern. They are basically the same as slogans and most people are aware of the power of slogans.

When a slogan is used with a instrumental jingle it has a long range effect. Some people have reported still remembering the following jingle as used in a 1960's toothpaste commercial: "You'll wonder where the yellow went when you brush your teeth with Pepsi-dent." That thought has remained in certain people's minds for over 50 years. And in the case mentioned, it was not associated with any traumatic event – just a television commercial. Consider the force of a crafted lyric placed in the mind of a vulnerable brainwashing victim?

The victim does not have to listen to the programmed recordings more than one or two times before the underlying hypnotic script becomes impressed into the subconscious. Once this is done, the victim need only hear the music associated with the script – not the underlying hidden script itself any longer – to be affected by the command. She may have a sudden swell of intense passion for the subjugator when listening to the song under which this script had been programmed if that's what the command ordered. Just the music itself on an non-programmed recording will elicit the called for response. The subconscious will hear the commands at the mere sound of the specific melody.

Most people have certain songs with which they associate powerful memories which were acquired through normal life activities. The programmed scripts have just as powerful an impact on the subconscious.

This is critical to know when deprogramming a victim. Once he or she has escaped the physical confinement he had been subject to under the subjugator, the victim will most likely listen to his favorite music again and be overcome by the underlying script that had been branded into the subconscious. It will continue to function no matter where the desecrated music is heard even on a recording which does not have the physical programming underlying it. The subconscious has already memorized the script and attached it permanently to the melody! The question to ask when deprogramming is basically – how to un-ring this bell because if the melody or even parts of it are played back to the victim on voice message or in any other format it will have a mind controlling effect.

Music is subverted in another important way. Certain tunes will be played by the subjugator for the victim when experiencing times of trauma. Just as we remember the music that was playing in the background when delightful events occur in our lives, so too do we recall the melody playing in the background during the worst moments of our lives. The subjugator knows how to play these expertly when wishing to control his victim. Simply have her favorite music playing in the background when beating her...for her own good, of course.

False Victories/Escapes

One of the most devious and successful tactics used in brainwashing is the periodic introduction to the victim of the sense of having escaped the mind control of his "captor" by allowing him to leave either physically or psychically. This is widely used among intelligence agencies and is certainly part of any competent subjugator's list of psychological weapons. This involves intermittent reinforcement at its most devastating. And it is one of the primary reasons why the victim is allowed to periodically return "home" after the initial stay of intense indoctrination.

Once at home, the victim may develop a sense that he might actually be able to return to a "normal" life as it used to be. Misguided assistance given to him by his defender – unaware of the principles in this report – and others of the support group may help in the creation of this false feeling of victory – **normalcy**. It is an ingenious trap of mental confinement!

But if the victim has already undergone indoctrination and brainwashing, why would he even think of escape? Because, for one reason or another, he is addicted to his subjugator. Remember that one thing almost all addicts have in common is a subconscious hatred for the object of their addiction? On that subconscious level, the victim seeks escape. When he is released from physical custody he naturally will sense that possibility of escape now. And the proficient subjugator knows this and how powerful intermittent reinforcement is.

Another reason that the victim is released from custody is to act as type of agent for the head of the cult or group and to help spread his doctrine. Maybe even to eventually convert you and others of the former support group. Remember, you and the others are also targets of brainwashing and control and the leader of this group feels he is beyond any harm from anyone.

I Become You

This is one of the least understood and most secretive of brainwashing techniques because it occurs deep in the subconscious and it is such a subtle, but insidious, process that even the victim does not know it has occurred. His thought pattern (subjugator's) has gradually become her (victim's) thought pattern. The victim's only hint that this has occurred is a suspicion that the subjugator can read her mind, her thoughts, and this imbues the manipulator with even greater miraculous powers in her mind.

The primary vehicle for applying this type of control is sleep deprivation and re-engineering REM sleep when it is allowed to occur. Keep in mind, the subjugator is probably of genius intellect and is devious in application of mind control.

The process itself is relatively simple. It involves the repeated use of the phrase, "You know that yourself..." concerning various topics while the victim is in a state of half slumber or otherwise deprived of sleep. It is a common practice used by propagandists to convince listeners that an idea or a point of data is such common knowledge that, "You know that yourself." Or that it is assumed that the listener accepts whatever the premise is. This has a powerful effect on the vulnerable mind, or even the inattentive hearer. You know that yourself.

One of the suggestions that the subjugator repeatedly implants in his victim's mind, but mostly during periods of altered mental states, is "You know how much you really love me." This idea is also subliminally appearing under musical pieces the victim listens to and in photo-shopped images. And what this does is take the victim's sense of I out of the equation and substitutes it with you, which removes her identity and replaces it with the subjugator's identity. "You know how much you really love me," is his command which she must obey and believe.

This applies to all other facets of the victim's life and the loss of personality. Her thoughts have become, "You like this type of food." "You thought that movie was great." "You accept whatever HE tells you as absolute truth." HE of course being the subjugator.

Loss of personality, identity and will.

Fake "Gurus" & "Spiritual Leaders"

As of the writing of this book, the cyber world and other venues for mass communication is crowded with fake "gurus" and so-called "spiritual leaders." The overwhelming majority of these people are con men. This includes so-called "channelers" or those who are supposedly in contact with higher intelligence.

Most of the "gurus" and "spiritual leaders" are male and their tactics are basically the same. One of their chief goals is to attract pretty young women to their following, invite them to their center (home) and then force sexual relations on them, claiming that they are transmitting the power of god into them. Many of these con men fake an East Indian background, or schooling, or pedigree, which provides them with 2 benefits. The first is an instant authority because so many people believe that all mystical thought originated in India. And secondly, it grants them the camouflage of a foreign culture of which most Westerners are not deeply knowledgeable, allowing the con men to claim special and bizarre rights of respect often including submission of a sexual nature.

While the "gurus" are almost exclusively men, the channelers are usually women. Many claim to be in direct contact with Jesus. Some speak to aliens. Others speak to powerful avatars. None of them offer any solid proof that their information comes from anywhere but their own imaginations.

These con men and con women charge high fees for their services and this is the primary reason for their practices. The male con men have the extra benefit of free sexual relations with whatever female – in some cases male – they can attract to their "causes."

Beware the fake "gurus." "spiritual leaders," and channelers. They will not show you any more mercy than your typical con man.

PART 2
REVERSAL/RECOVERY

1. Introduction
2. Reclaiming A Relationship
3. Revealing Hypnotic Control
4. Changing the Tune
5. Exposing An Enemy
6. Break the Grip of Sex
7. You Become I Again
8. Stalemate
9. Confound the Enemy
10. The Final Stage

Introduction

What follows is to be used to deprogram the victim once the initial indoctrination/brainwashing visit to the subjugator has taken place. True brainwashing must almost always be performed while the subject is in custody. There are rare instances in which the victim remained at his or her domicile and was there brainwashed while subjected to tortuous hours of indoctrination and humiliation while frozen to the computer screen using Skype and other systems of visual and verbal communication. This is extremely rare.

However, Optimal damage to the subject can only be perpetrated in person while the victim is basically held hostage – whether violently or not. Even psychologically being held hostage is terrifying.

What can be done to help the victim once he or she has been ostensibly released from bondage and has returned home or near home? That's what you will be shown now and much of it is based on US intelligence agency procedures of a non-classified nature.

Part 2 will be different from part 1 in presentation. In this section, a specific technique of brainwashing or other type of mind control will be highlighted and then the action that could be taken to neutralize it will be given. In part I the methods used in mind control and the reasoning supporting their use have been given so that in part 2 the manner of unraveling them can be provided and understandably explained.

Recall that brainwashing is accomplished through repetition and under intense pressure while the subject is held in some type of custody. The control that is placed upon the subject's mind remains even after he is allowed to leave and return to public.

Removing this control of the victim's mind is also done over a period of time but minus the pressure of being in custody. Removing the power of brainwashing is like removing the mystery of a magic trick – revealing how it is done!

One of the primary ways to neutralize brainwashing is by subtly demonstrating the process of brainwashing to the victim but without the intent of brainwashing the victim yourself. You must demonstrate to the victim how his mind was taken over by enacting in a non-threatening or judgmental way examples of how it was done. As noted earlier, in order to do this, you need to know how it was done yourself, and much of this has already been presented to you. At this point in the book, specific neutralizing applications come into play. These are suggestions for how you might react to the situation before you now. Remember, all situations are different and one single method will not be successful for all.

What to do after the victim has returned "home" or has returned to the area. It is possible that yours may be one of those cases in which the victim shuttles back and forth over periods of time between his former "home" and the lair of the subjugator.

Reclaiming A Relationship

The subjugtor has succeeded in disrupting the relationship between you and the victim through hypnosis and brainwashing. The victim has returned "home" from her indoctrination for an indefinite time. One of your first priorities is to attempt to restore the relationship that once existed between you.

(The specific actions to be taken can be altered to reflect the particular type of relation that exists between victim and defender. The original case involved a romantically involved pair).

Note the title of this section. It is Reclaiming **A** relationship in a non-definitive way, meaning not any specific type of relationship, because what formerly had existed may be temporarily or even permanently lost. Your plan at this point is to redevelop a civil relationship during which you will be able to institute the procedures that neutralize brainwashing. It is important to start slowly and as diplomatically as possible. If you are not viewed specifically as an enemy you are at best only a neutral bystander to the victim at this point.

ACTION TAKEN: The friend or loved one is innocently and clearly asked: "What was really the condition of our relationship before you became involved in this (group)? I don't recall it being that bad."

Yes, that is what is asked. Does this seem too simple? Sometimes, that's precisely what's needed. It is a question that in these cases vitally needs to be asked but almost never is.

Soon after my friend came under hypnotic assault by the subjugator we began to have periodic arguments. These grew increasingly more serious and more often. My friend would say that she was getting more and more involved with the subjugator because our relationship was more and more quickly deteriorating. "We were fighting all the time anyway," she insisted. "That's why I turned away and eventually left."

Initially, even I believed that. I came under the same delusion that the subjugator had created. But something always bothered me about the idea that my friend and I were not getting along at that time: my subconscious knew this wasn't true. Every time it would be claimed that we were fighting and not getting along anyway I felt a twinge of discomfort. Because it wasn't true! At least not at the beginning.

Maybe ours wasn't the perfect relationship but it was far from being a hostile one at the beginning. Why does this matter? Because realizing what happened to destroy a relationship is the beginning of exposing the effects of brainwashing.

I noted to my friend that I knew that I had come under almost constant attack by the subjugator and that this had had a great impact on her view of me and us. When she said something to the effect, "You know, that's right," deprogramming her seemed feasible. She was able to open her mind enough to see some truth of the situation. We weren't relating badly at all when she began her contact with the subjugator.

This isn't to say that the victim immediately agreed with my observation. But I was surprised how quickly she did see the reality of it after I'd asked that basic question a number of times.

This tactic may not necessary be successful for you if you did really have a contentious relationship before the subjugator inserted himself into it. However, even under this condition it might help, showing how his influence increased and intensified any hostilities.

Deprogramming is a lengthy and uncertain process. For three steps forward, you may fall two steps backward. Especially if the subjugator maintains ANY contact with his victim, which you may not be able to control. Remember, the victim is addicted to the subjugator and the only way to end an addiction is total abstinence. And this includes text messages, voice messages, emails and any other form of contact. While just receiving one of these types of communique may not be enough to cause descent into full scale addiction again after abstinence, it would represent a freshly poured glass of alcohol placed before a recovered alcoholic! And the subjugator knows this.

Like all addictions, the addict himself must choose freedom from it. The way can be shown, but he must ultimately decide.

Revealing Hypnotic Control

A critical part of deprogramming, is demonstrating to the victim how hypnosis was used to control him. Once the trick is exposed, the victim will be more willing to accept your warnings about brainwashing and how his mind was stolen from him.

This, too, will be a multi-stage process and will occur over an indeterminate period of time. Recall that all aspects of deprogramming occur simultaneously in much the same way as brainwashing was performed.

ACTION TAKEN: Re-enactment of certain types of hypnotic events or brainwashing actions that the victim has alluded to and described to you himself (probably without his knowledge). The purpose being to reveal to the victim the powerful effects brainwashing has on a vulnerable person and exposing this portion of the mind control trick.

When a person is subjecting another person to hypnotic suggestions during a conversation, the subjugator almost always uses some form of object to distract the mind of the victim so that the psychic impressions proceed more fluently and easily into his subconscious. The subjugator may continually twist the chain of a necklace he is wearing, flip some type of handheld object back and forth in his grasp, or simply repeatedly tug on the band of a watch or other pieces of jewelry. This is probably what happened when the subjugator used hypnosis on the victim. The victim may have even described her talks with him and unknowingly or unwittingly depicted his distracting use of various objects. He may have even played with the locks of his hair. Anything to distract the listener's mind.

During deprogramming, one of the surest ways to contact the subconscious mind of the victim is to casually – subtly – re-enact some of these hypnotic sessions, hopefully using in real time the same type of item that the subjugator used for distraction during brainwashing.

Re-enacting the hypnotic conversation before the victim – she witnessing the event – while you use another person as the other party of the discussion, can be quite effective. However, it is extremely difficult to do this without the purpose of the act being obvious to the observer. But it is a risk worth taking because the sight of seeing someone under mild hypnotic attack might jar the subconscious so that realization is accomplished.

It is useful even should the victim become enraged by your performance of what a hypnotic attack would look like from an observer's point of view. Can the observer – in this case the victim – simply ignore that this type of activity had occurred to her? And once it is realized that it had occurred, what effect does that have? Few people react positively to being subjected to hypnotic suggestion. But few people easily admit to it as having happened to them.

Another way to present this view of hypnotic control to the victim is to make it seem a positive action – something that is done for a subject's benefit. Suggest that since the subjugator is so far advanced over "normal" people, it might be a good idea for him to control the lives of others for their own good. Will the victim see the absurdity of this idea? At any rate, bringing the idea of hypnotic domination into discussion is the immediate objective.

Changing the Tune

Has music been used to brainwash the victim? Test his or her reaction when listening to various pieces of music, particularly those suggested by the victim which are most likely her favorites. If there is positive proof of brainwashing, a possible neutralization may lie in repeated, continuous playbacks to the victim of an uncontaminated version of the compromised music in order to lessen or remove the impact of the subliminal commands.

In part I of this book, it was noted what a powerful role music could play in the act of brainwashing. Has the victim with whom you are working been subject to brainwashing through music, either by being controlled by subliminal messages underneath the melody or by trauma associated with hearing a particular melody? One way to discover if this is the case is to spend time with her when she is listening to music, particularly her favorite pieces.

Simply note any strange or unusual reactions the victim has when the suspect music is playing. Less obvious are the residual effects it might have afterwards once the music has stopped.

Or else note how the victim's reactions to various musicians, composers or musical bands in general may have changed – sometimes drastically. Bands that may once have been a favorite are now listened to with distaste, etc.

ACTION TAKEN: Listen with the victim to as many of his or her favorite musical recordings as feasible. If there is positive proof of brainwashing using subliminal commands underlying musical recordings, a possible neutralization may lie in repeated playbacks to the victim of uncontaminated versions of the compromised music. This may result, if playback is done to excess, in diminishing the power of the brainwashing commands by a process similar to "flooding" which causes the offending words to lose their psychic corrosiveness and to decrease their power to harm the victim.

This is among the most difficult and pernicious of brainwashing effects to neutralize. It is particularly insidious in that by overwriting musical melodies that once provided happiness to the listener these same tunes now offer dark commands created by the subjugator to the subconscious of the victim. The listener now is made uneasy, even angry, by the once joyful melodies and develops a hostile association with the people whom she shares them with (listening to them with you).

These altered musical tracts may also be transformed into almost an inspiration theme, however. Consider the idea that a once cherished tune is suddenly annoying to the victim. But, upon hearing another special command implanted into the recording – the name of the subjugator – a feeling of joyousness overcomes the victim. Almost magically, his name alone has returned the feeling of pleasure once associated with this defiled melody. Much in the way great relief pours over the citizens in the classic movie "1984" when the photo of Big Brother is flashed before them in the midst of a traumatic scene. This tactic could be applied only to one of the victim's beloved pieces of music, though. The rest that have been defiled will retain their ugliness.

There is one certain way to break the subjugator's control of the contaminated musical tracts. That would happen if a copy of one of the altered recordings with the subliminal commands could be obtained and these commands made audible to the victim. But since this is essentially not ever likely to happen, the more painstaking method of extinguishing these subliminal commands as suggested above is one of the best possibilities. Other than having the victim abandon his or he favorite music. It is, as noted, unlikely that the subjugator would apply his subliminal implants to music the victim seldom listened to.

Clinical hypnosis undertaken by a qualified hypnotist may also be used to remove the effects of the contaminated music. This would be extremely costly, time consuming and potentially ineffective.

A similar form of hypnotic control could be used against the victim by using paintings or photographs as the medium of control. The subjugator verbally implants commands into the victim's subconscious while discussing and viewing a painting of particular interest. This can be applied to any other form of visual display.

This type of subliminal control was often used by advertising agencies in the past, particularly by the liquor industry. Hideous scenes of death and destruction were depicted by being drawn within the forms of the ice cubes in the liquor glasses used by the imbibers. This was supposed to interact with the self destructive impulses of alcoholics and others of that nature who were prone to use liquor frequently. The same concept was used in cigarette advertisements. This type of advertising was supposedly made illegal. Brainwashing, of course, does not recognize this type of restriction.

Visual brainwashing can be very powerful. But it has limitations because the medium on which the subliminal images are produced often has to be repeatedly shown to the victim which creates suspicion. This aspect of mind control is noted for completeness and in the event the victim may have artistic knowledge and interests. In this case, the types of control just noted might be more frequently used and may be highly effective.

Exposing An Enemy

A critical part of deprogramming is pointing out the enemy without directly accusing him as being the enemy. At this stage, the more subtle subterfuges that were used by the subjugator to control the victim are tactfully described and demonstrated to the victim. The purpose is to cause the victim to question the infallibility and special powers claimed by the subjugator and to realize that he can be identified as a fake because of his shared use of the same illusions and deceptions as other con men. What follows is a list of the most commonly shared "tricks" used by these con men/hucksters and brief explanations of their usage.

While it has been remarked how the stages of brainwashing are followed usually in the same pattern in all cases, it is also true that the specific techniques used during these stages of control by the subjugators is also very similar. In other words, they use the same types of tricks in the same way for the same purpose. Exposing this to the victim can be very powerful in getting him to see the reality of how he was placed under control – by design and through trickery by a con man. This realization often makes the victim annoyed or angry enough to try to free himself from the person who betrayed him by stealing his mind.

ACTION TAKEN: Reveal the various "tricks of the trade" used by the subjugator like all other con men.

TRICKS OF THE DECEIVERS

Fits of Crying

This activity hasn't been covered extensively but it is an important tactic used by many of the subjugators. Primarily to instill severe guilt in the victim, these egocentric maniacs brake down in uncontrollable fits of sobbing, often dropping to their knees in apparent prostration. The intensity of the crying and show of emotion overwhelms the victims who swear that this behavior by the subjugator cannot be faked. IT CAN BE AND IT IS FAKED.

There are many ways that a person can cause himself to sob uncontrollably on demand – some involve the use of a tear-inducing chemical; other methods are as simple as yanking a hair nose out of the inside of the nostrils. (The NSA even has a sonic method for inducing streams of tears). This out of control behavior can continue for any length of time which the subjugator deems sufficient to wear down the startled viewer with guilt, or whatever other emotion is desired.

There is also a psychotic physical condition associated with fits of uncontrollable sobbing from which the subjugator may suffer. It is similar to an opposite condition to which the subjugator is prone: fits of unrestrained laughter. Medical study has found that a defect in a certain part of the brain effects people who suffer from a specific type of insanity so that on particular provocation they laugh uncontrollably. So, there is a valid reason why Hollywood often depicts raving lunatics caught in the throes of fits of laughter. In any event, this isn't the type of person to whom I would entrust my allegiance or well being. Should the victim?

Incessant Talking

This is another activity that is used to break down the will of the victim. The subject matter doesn't necessarily matter, but the ceaseless relentlessness of verbal assault does matter. The constant bombardment of words eventually forces the mind of the hearer into submission so that whatever the subjugator wishes to impale the subconscious with will strike its target.

Demand for Loyalty

This is common among all so-called charismatic leaders. To ensure that their megalomaniacal, narcissistic needs are fully met they demand that all followers swear allegiance to them in one form or another. This implies that any other opposing viewpoints on the dogma that this cult, organization or club follows will be shunned and any other authority on the topic demonized. The victim is not allowed to change leaders under the threat of punishments induced through brainwashing and by the weight of unbearable guilt.

Enforced Inactivity

Have you ever waited in line at the DMV, or at a train depot, or an air terminal, or waited for anything else for such a length of time that it became almost physically painful? The subjugator is adept at inflicting this kind of enforced inactivity upon his victims. Not only does he force people to wait lengthy amounts of time for him to perform some type of action but he intermittently gives indication that the wait is finally over, but then halts proceedings again and causes another period of waiting. This causes an ever greater strain on the painfully "patient" victims – thinking the wait is finally over to be disappointed that it has resumed.

What's the purpose of this? CONTROL!

Bags Under the Eyes

This may be one of the most telltale signs of brainwashing, and yet the least likely that anyone would look for except a person who has had extensive direct experience with mind control. Bags under the victim's eyes – or the supposed lack of them. This is one of the stranger of commonalities found among people undergoing brainwashing and as such commonly used by their subjugators (all con men alike).

Bags under the eyes commonly develop after lengthy hours of wakefulness. Sleep deprivation is a common tactic used during brainwashing. In order to mask this condition, the subjugator gives the subconscious command to his victims that their eyes are clear and wide of appearance, despite the fact that they are bruised with bagginess. If you remark to a person who is undergoing brainwashing that her eyes look baggy for some reason she most likely will angrily deny it – despite the evidence to any viewer. The victim's subconscious will reveal a face in the mirror – free from baggy eyes – which the subjugator has decreed be seen.

The Astounding Miracle

As of this writing, every person whom I have sought to deprogram has claimed that the subjugator had won his devotion, or respect, or allegiance – whatever the term that fits – through the performance of some wondrous feat or miracle. Something so extraordinary that it convinced the viewer that the worker of this great miracle certainly had super human abilities and was due the highest form of honor and fear. So far, none of these "witnesses" has ever described what the great miracle was. None of them.

The purpose in presenting this section is to reveal some of the more typical "tricks of the trade" to use a common term, that are employed by these "gurus," inspired leaders, personages of power or by whatever description the subjugators of other person's wills wish to describe themselves. Basically, they are all con men and use the same misdirection and deceit to invade the minds of unsuspecting and usually trusting victims.

Break the Grip of Sex

If the brainwashing involves a male subjugator and a female victim, sexual activity is almost certainly an element involved in the mind control procedure. The act of sex binds the female victim to the subjugator both through shame and guilt, but usually only if she had a relationship with another male before succumbing to the subjugator. Otherwise, she will be bound by the basic power of the subjugator's force, control and virility and, as already noted, may fall in love with him or be made to believe she is in love with him. This is a special form of control which is consciously used by the subjugator and is exceptionally difficult to overcome by both the victim and the defender (you).

It isn't unusual for a female victim to be induced into sexual relations with the subjugator while in his custody. Even if she has a husband or other sweetheart whom she'd been separated from by hypnotic suggestion. I am not currently aware of cases where a female subjugator has forced sexual relations on a male subject otherwise these would have been included here. This doesn't mean they don't exist, just that they are exceptionally rare.

In cases where a female victim is induced into sexual relations it is seldom a one-time occurrence and is probably a regular event. If this is a situation where the subjugator claims to be a "guru" or spiritual leader with special powers, his primary argument is that he is bestowing the spirit of God upon his victim through intimate contact. This is actually part of many of the "belief systems" of many of these so-called spiritual cults.

ACTION TAKEN: FOCUS ON THE REAL ENEMY! He is the one who is ultimately guilty. He is the one who is ultimately to blame.

If sexual contact has been part of the brainwashing assault it will certainly be one of the most difficult aspects of deprogramming with which to deal, both for the victim and the defender. If you are emotionally involved with the victim it will be almost humanly impossible to maintain a helpful attitude toward the victim who agreed to take part in the sexual activity with the subjugator. But you can! I do not state this lightly or as a mere hope. As has been noted several times the information in this report is **FROM PERSONAL EXPERIENCE** and not mere theory or speculation.

Unfortunately, it wasn't until after the fact that I

became aware that the first victim I eventually helped was brainwashed. At this point I was educated by friends in the US Intelligence agencies about deprogramming methods and how I could rescue this close friend of mine from the madman who'd taken control of her mind.

It is easy to blame the victim for getting involved with the subjugator at the outset. But did she intend to be subjected to brainwashing?

No one has the right to force brainwashing on another person, no matter what errors of judgment the victim initially made. The enemy is the subjugator.

You Become I Again

The victim will claim to love the subjugator. This may even be true. But is it a true love or a hypnotically induced love? This is one of the most difficult questions to answer. The primary problem is that the victim will not even know the answer. That's what the subjugator expects.

But does the subjugator love the victim? Almost definitely not. The subjugator is a narcissistic psychopath whose only concern is for himself. He doesn't have the ability to love anyone else. What he wants is admiration and unqualified devotion.

After deprogramming has been in progress for awhile and has made progress something unsuspected might happen. The victim may say something like this to you in a desperate voice: "I love him. I really do love him. But I want to get him out of my head. Help me get him out of my head!" This is a series of agonized remarks that I have experienced in real life. It isn't fiction.

How to respond to these seemingly contradictory remarks from the victim?

There is one vital clue here and the only one that will be given by the victim. If she **TRULY** loves the subjugator, why does she so desperately want to get him out of her head? It's as if the subconscious is reaching out directly and claiming that the type of love induced in the victim isn't genuine but artificial.

"I love him. I really do love him. But I want to get him out of my head. Help me get him out of my head!"

How do you get the subjugator out of her head?

First – how did he get into her head? The answer refers back to the chapter on pronoun substitution – **I Become You**. That is how he got into her head and how he remains there. It is a particularly pernicious and tenacious posthypnotic command that required great effort upon the part of the subjugator to implant. In fact, he probably geared all tactics – sleep deprivation, nutrition deprivation, humiliation, sexual control, etc. – to firmly perform the pronoun substitution.

The primary weapon in this case would be sleep deprivation and re-engineering REM sleep when it is allowed to occur.

Recall that pronoun substitution is the process whereby the victim believes her thoughts are originating from an outside source. This outside source is the subjugator. So, when she tells you, "I love him," concerning the subjugator, the words that actually occur in her mind are, "You love him." Or, more accurately, as in the section I BECOME YOU, "You know that you really do love him." This was implanted by the subjugator. That's how her love for him got into her head and how he got into her head.

How do you remove him? You don't. Only the victim can. But you can provide critical advice on how the exorcism can take place. The victim must become aware that the intruder inside of her head forced himself into her mind by subterfuge with the plan of taking over her will. Remind her again of all the specific ways he has worn down her self respect, her sense of identity and her view of reality.

While it is critically important when the victim notices that someone else is directing her thoughts, do not expect this to be final. The next day she may tell you directly that she never asked you for help in "getting him out of my head." Expect this to happen. But it isn't a reason to give up. It marks another one of those false victories, but not a defeat!

Stalemate

You have spent a great deal of time implementing the deprogramming procedures in this book. You have demonstrated to the victim how the subjugator used hypnotic suggestion to overcome him. You have highlighted the forms of brainwashing that the subjugator has used to gain possession of the victim. There have been numerous false escapes and victories: times when the victim has seemed to see clearly how badly she had been mistreated only to fall back into the darkness of subjection. The amount of progress that has been made has been equally offset by the same amount of backsliding. After many months of work you have come to a stalemate.

The victim still is unsure if she really loves her subjugator or not. She still isn't sure if he is a fraud or an enlightened (awakened) master. She is still debating whether or not she should return to his ashram, compound or complex and maybe remain permanently. All that remains are doubts which have been caysed by all of the evidence that you have presented. But the one emotion binding the victim to the subjugator now is that feeling of love. Is it real? Is it not? It is a stalemate that only the victim can decide.

If the deprogramming involves a male addicted to a charismatic personality, he is no longer certain whether or not this leader is truly as powerful as he claims. Is this someone he should really continue to rely on and support? He is uncertain if this is the infallible leader he once believed him to be or just a...con man?

In any case, the stalemate has occurred because the victim is now balancing between escape from or continued reverence to the subjugator.

Confound the Enemy

It was stated earlier in this report that one of the strongest weapons that you – the defender – may have against the enemy is confusion. Do something that confounds him, something he cannot fully understand. And while he is struggling with his bewilderment he will make mistakes that he hadn't made before when he was in total control of himself. At this time, the victim is having a chance to decide if her love for him is truly real. Or how strong the addiction is.

Remember, from the subjugator's point of view you are the enemy – one of the victim's support group whom he believes has already been discredited to the victim. As such, the subjugator expects you to continue to bear animosity toward him and to continue to speak negatively about him to the victim. But suppose you instead claimed to want to give the VICTIM the benefit of a doubt in this matter and listen to his arguments and philosophy after all. Only the victim's opinions on this topic matter and you will abide with her decision.

At first this would fill the subjugtor with great pride at seemingly being victorious over you. But being a narcissistic megalomaniac he would've expected you to at some point admit defeat since only he matters and always has deserved unreserved adulation. However, possessing the personality that he does, this new situation is totally bewildering to him. How does he treat you now since you are giving his chosen victim leeway to make up her own mind? Should he, the subjugator, continue to treat you with hostility? Or should he be magnanimous and treat you as a nebulous, new convert?

And, of course, is this all a trick you are playing on him the subjugator might ask himself. Is your sudden capitulation to the wishes of his victim a ruse to take the subjugator off guard? But to what end? He has placed his victim under his firm control. He knows that because the victim is still in contact with him, the subjugator's trigger commands are still activated, and the victim has even told him she is still devoted to him. What should he fear? After all, he is invincible in his own mind.

You, the reader, are probably very confused right now. So was I when I was first presented with this tactic by technicians of the US intelligence agency with whom I deal.

But this is a psychologically engineered tactic. It is meant to reach directly into the victim's subconscious and open it up to all possibilities – even that she may have been duped by her master, the subjugator.

I can't explain precisely how this works. And I cannot take credit for originating it. When I told my associates about the stalemate situation after more than 12 months of battle this seemingly simple solution was prescribed. It is only SEEMINGLY simple. It is a mental deflection that re-arranges all aspects of the situation. A judo move. A sidestep to the left which puts everyone off balance – to a purpose!

And during this new stage of confrontation, you never contact the subjugator directly, but all communication is done through the victim.

Have you truly capitulated? In one sense you have. You have come to realize that there is a possibility that the victim may truly have a deep emotional connection of one form or another with the subjugator. For a person to be released from mind control the victim must truly desire to be freed from it. He may not always want that for himself, even if you do. Forcing this choice on the victim is the ultimate option. He or she will decide; you are giving the option.

At this point, you are acting out of total consideration for the victim. You have to extinguish all of your own beliefs in this matter. You have to accept the fact that if you really care for the victim – no matter your relationship, even a spouse – you may have to risk losing him or her. You have to expand your humanity and sensibility, possibly far beyond it has ever been before. To gain something you must often be willing to let go of it entirely and have faith in the outcome. This is where the stalemate has brought you and the victim and the subjugator. You, too, are in the web. But you have one commodity the other 2 may not fully possess any longer - freedom of choice.

Also recall from an earlier remark that it would be almost impossible to know if the victim is truly in love with the subjugator (in male/female situations). The just laid out strategy is one of the possible ways to learn this. It will create a conflict in the subconscious of the victim which will cause the genuine feelings to come to the fore by casting you in a different light.

Why not force this issue earlier? Because it has dangerous consequences and is something of a last resort once all else has resulted in a stalemate. Also, it is critical that all of the facts of brainwashing be exposed so that the victim will be able to use this as a factor in deciding his true feelings for the subjugator.

Action like this will also effect the addicted status of the victim in ways difficult to predict. It may even free her to hate even more forcefully the control of her addiction to the subjugator and in a sense bestow a certain type of freedom on the victim. Or it may make the addiction to this person even more appealing: women are attracted to him because of his sensuality, men are attracted to his sense of power which they hope to share through him. The anticipated effect of the action taken here by the defender is to allow for a break in the stalemate for everyone involved.

And it is important to repeat: this can only be done now after the victim has been shown the evidence of the mind control wielded by the subjugator.

At any rate, he next move is up to the victim.

The Final Stage

The final stage in taking complete control of the victim is by co-opting his or her finances - the subjugator's combining the victim's monetary resources with his own. While this is usually done when the victim is already in "permanent residence" with the subjugator, the plans for it often take place prior to the victim's final parting with friends and loved ones. All of the transfer of resources through the banks, brokerage houses and other financial institutions are often completed before last departure. The subjugator wants to be certain that he has control of the funds before taking full physical control of the victim.

This can be done in privacy, no matter the victim's relationship to you, the defender. Be assured that the subjugator has access to some of the best legal and accounting professionals in the business.

This final stage may be instigated by your apparent loosening of your defense posture. The subjugator may decide that this is a sign that all protection has been removed from the victim and he can "move in for the kill," for want of a better term. And this implies taking control of the victim's finances which will bring him completely under the subjugator's domination.

How the victim reacts will probably determine the outcome to this entire brainwashing event. Ultimately, with all the facts in his or her possession, it is the victim's choice. You have done the best you could do – guide the victim to the best decision in his or her own interest.

Remember what was noted at the beginning, the final outcome of deprogramming must be directed toward what is in the VICTIM'S own best interest which may not be the same conclusion which you would prefer to see.

APPENDIX 1

CRISIS POINTS

These are critical points of danger during the implementation of mind control and if neutralized may halt the progress of indoctrination.

1. INTRODUCTION OF HYPNOSIS

Occurs at an early direct contact between victim and subjugator, either in person or through any other medium, visual or otherwise A simple process during which the subjugator introduces himself as the victim's friend and benefactor who can be trusted to have only the victim's interests in mind. This begins and sets the stage for the "relationship" that follows.

2. FIRST WARNING SIGNS - VICTIM'S FIXATION ON A SPECIFIC TOPIC, INTEREST, OR PERSON TO THE EXCLUSION OF ALL ELSE. (aka Monomania).

Inject yourself forcefully into the victim's life right now to break the pattern of monomania or it may be far in the future if ever when you will be able to mentally contact him or her again. (pages 20-24).

3. VICTIM'S EXAGGERATED RAGE OVER SEEMINGLY MINOR MATTERS.

The victim suddenly explodes with exaggerated rage over what normally are minor annoyances that have existed between both of you through most of your relationship. These have been elevated into serious battles by the subjugator through his stealthily introduced hypnotic suggestions to the victim and incessant picking away at her thoughts. (pages 27-28)

4. ATTACK OF SILENCE

All verbal communication between you and the victim breaks down at the subjugator's direction and insistence. This is usually the final stage before the victim physically departs. Drastic action is needed at this point and close vigilance of the victim MUST be maintained. (pages 30 – 31).

5. CYBER DEVASTATION

A cyber hacker working for the subjugator infiltrates your cyber network and delivers to the victim a heinous message seemingly sent from you which will cause the victim to depart instantly in a rage. (pages 34 – 37).

6. DEPARTURE/GONE

The victim leaves either with or without warning and – either way – you are suddenly left alone with the least amount of information about his or her whereabouts, most if not all of which is useless and a fabrication. You can no longer trust ANYTHING that the victim has told you because he is now loyal only to the head of the cult, group or secret organization. (pages 40 – 42).

7. FORCING A RESPONSE (CRITICAL)

The victim has departed home and has not been heard from for over 2 weeks with the possible exception of scantily devised text messages of one form or another. All verbal contact has been denied. Nothing is known of his or her whereabouts.

ACTION TAKEN: At this point, I knew that extreme measures are to be used because all else has failed. A powerful and extremely forceful message was sent to the victim by email. This message is **NOT** to be sent by anyone who has already previously attempted contact. No matter it's content it would probably be ignored outright if sent by any of these people.

The message is to be sent by an interested "third party" who knows the victim and is closely associated with members of her family and/or support group. It could be a relative or even a spouse of a child of the victim's. The major requirement is that this person has not yet tried to contact the victim and that he is well acquainted with the victim in one way or another.

CONTENT OF THE MESSAGE: It must be severe and strike directly at the inhumane way in which the victim is treating friends and loved ones. It must not use euphemisms – mild alternative descriptions – but clear, exact, shocking language in order to get the full attention of the victim and subjugator. The message must begin powerfully and without apology.

APPENDIX 2

QUICK GUIDE OF RECOVERY AND REVERSAL METHODS FOR IMMEDIATE USE

Reclaiming A Relationship

The subjugator has succeeded in disrupting the relationship between you and the victim through hypnosis and brainwashing. The victim has returned "home" from her indoctrination for an indefinite time. One of the first priorities is to attempt to restore the relationship that once existed between you.

ACTION TAKEN: The friend or loved one is innocently and clearly asked: "What was really the condition of our relationship before you became involved in this (group)? I don't recall it being that bad."

Revealing Hypnotic Control

A critical part of deprogramming, is demonstrating to the victim how hypnosis was used to control him. Once the trick is exposed, the victim will be more willing to accept your warnings about brainwashing and how his mind was stolen from him.

ACTION TAKEN: Re-enacting certain types of hypnotic events or brainwashing actions that the victim has alluded to and described to you himself (probably without his knowledge). The purpose being to reveal the powerful effects this has on a vulnerable person and exposing this portion of the brainwashing trick.

Changing the Tune

Has music been used to brainwash the victim? Test his or her reaction when listening to various pieces of music, particularly those suggested by the victim which are most likely her favorites. If there is positive proof of brainwashing, a possible neutralization may lie in repeated, continuous playbacks to the victim of an uncontaminated version of the compromised music in order to lessen or remove the impact of the subliminal commands.

ACTION TAKEN: Listening with the victim to as many of his or her favorite musical recordings as feasible. If there is positive proof of brainwashing, using subliminal commands underlying musical recordings, a possible neutralization may lie in repeated playbacks to the victim of uncontaminated versions of the compromised music. This may result, if playback is done to excess, in diminishing the power of the brainwashing commands by a similar process to what was commonly known as "flooding" which causes the offending words to lose their psychic corrosiveness and to decrease their power to harm.

Exposing An Enemy

A critical part of deprogramming is pointing out the enemy without directly accusing him as being the enemy. At this time, the tricks that were used by the subjugator to control the victim are subtly described and demonstrated to the victim. The purpose is to cause the victim to question the infallibility and special powers claimed by the subjugator and to realize that he can be identified as a fake because of his shared use of the same illusions and deceptions as other con men.

ACTION TAKEN: Revealing and describing the "tricks of the trade" that this subjugator shares with other con men of his type.

Break the Grip of Sex

If the brainwashing involves a male subjugator and a female victim, sexual activity is almost certainly an element involved in the mind control procedure. The act of sex binds the female victim to the subjugator both through shame and guilt, but usually only if she had a relationship with another male before succumbing to the subjugator. Otherwise, she will be bound by the basic power of the subjugator's force, control and virility and, as already noted, may fall in love with him or be made to believe she is in love with him. This is a special form of control which is consciously used by the subjugator and is exceptionally difficult to overcome by both the victim and the defender (you).

ACTION TAKEN: FOCUS ON THE REAL ENEMY! He is the one who is ultimately guilty. He is the one who is ultimately to blame.

You Become I Again

The victim will claim to love the subjugator. This may even be true. But is it a true love or a hypnotically induced love? This is one of the most difficult questions to answer. The primary problem is that the victim will not even know the true answer. That's what the subjugator wants.

Remember, this series of remarks: "I love him. I really do love him. But I want to get him out of my head. Help me get him out of my head!" This is not fiction but actual spoken words.

ACTION TAKEN: Recalling that pronoun substitution is the process whereby the victim is made to believe that her thoughts are believed to be originating from an outside source. This outside source is the subjugator. So, when she tells you, "I love him," concerning the subjugator, the words that actually occur in her mind are, "You love him." Or, more accurately, as in the section I BECOME YOU, "You know that you really do love me." as implanted by the subjugator. That's how her love for him got into her head and how he got into her head. Try to explain this to the victim.

Stalemate

You have spent a great deal of time implementing the deprogramming instructions in this book. You have demonstrated to the victim how the subjugator used hypnotic suggestion to overcome him. You have highlighted the forms of brainwashing that the subjugator has used to gain possession of the victim. There have been numerous false escapes and victories: times when the victim has seemed to see clearly how badly she had been

mistreated only to fall back into the darkness of subjection. The amount of progress that has been made has been equally offset by the same amount of backsliding. After many months of work you have come to a stalemate.

ACTION TAKEN: Confounding the enemy by giving in unconditionally to all the requests of the **victim**. Let him or her follow whatever fate they choose and truly accept the decision. The subjugator will not expect this and will begin making mistakes due to his confusion over how to act when someone who is considered an outsider, an enemy – which is you – agrees with him and his victim with their chosen plans. At this point, you must be willing to do what the victim feels is in his or her best interests.

Made in the USA
Middletown, DE
27 January 2024

48506598R00082